Developing Everyday Coping Skills in the Early Years

A companion website to accompany this book is available online at:

http://education.frydenberg2.continuumbooks.com

Please type in the URL above and receive your unique password for access to the book's online resources.

If you experience any problems accessing the resources, please contact Continuum at: info@continuumbooks.com

Also available from Continuum

Think Positively!, Erica Frydenberg

The Thinking Child, Nicola Call and Sally Featherstone

The Thinking Child Resource Book (2nd edition), Nicola Call and
    Sally Featherstone

100 Ideas for Teaching Knowledge and Understanding of the World,
    Alan Thwaites

Developing Everyday Coping Skills in the Early Years

Proactive Strategies for Supporting Social and Emotional Development

Erica Frydenberg, Jan Deans
and Kelly O'Brien

B L O O M S B U R Y
LONDON · NEW DELHI · NEW YORK · SYDNEY

Published 2012 by Continuum
an imprint of Bloomsbury Publishing Plc
50 Bedford Square, London W1B 3DP

www.bloomsbury.com

ISBN: 978-1-4411-6104-8 (paperback)
      978-1-4411-6010-2 (ePub)
      978-1-4411-8799-4 (PDF)

First published 2012 by Continuum International Publishing Group
Reprinted 2012

A CIP record for this publication is available from the British Library.

Typeset by Newgen Imaging Systems Pvt Ltd, Chennai, India
Printed and bound in Great Britain

This book is produced using paper that is made from wood grown in
managed, sustainable forests. It is natural, renewable and recyclable. The
logging and manufacturing processes conform to the environmental
regulations of the country of origin.

Contents

Acknowledgements

The authors would like to acknowledge the support of staff and students at the University of Melbourne Early Learning Centre and Toorak College, Mt Eliza for the opportunity to trial the ideas in this book and to receive feedback.

In addition we would like to acknowledge the support provided by the University of Melbourne, a stimulating environment for creative endeavours and the grant provided by the R. E. Trust that enabled this publication to be completed.

Finally we would like to acknowledge the support from Continuum UK, particularly from Melanie Wilson who encouraged us to produce this volume.

Introduction

An overview of social and emotional development

Social and emotional competence underpins healthy development, educational achievement and the well-being of a community. Coping skills are an important index of such competence. Finding the best ways to promote productive coping in children and those around them is our challenge. Nevertheless research on coping has helped us to understand what to teach and what not to teach and which are the elements in early years' settings that enable the development of everyday coping skills for healthy social and emotional development.

Social and emotional competence includes key qualities which, when put into practice, produce socially and emotionally healthy and productive individuals, as well as safe and responsive communities. These qualities include reflection and empathy, flexible and creative problem solving and decision making, control of impulses, clear and direct communication and self-motivation. There is a significant body of research demonstrating a strong link between social and emotional well-being and learning and the critical role of social and emotional development across the life span. The research (Durlak et al., 2011; Zins et al., 2004) indicates that:

- there is evidence that these skills can be taught during the P-12 years;
- students participating in effective social and emotional education programmes characteristically engage in less self-destructive and disruptive behaviour and in more positive social behaviour; and
- students often show improvements in their academic performances.

There are key bodies in the international community that are engaged in this enterprise. These include the Collaborative for Academic, Social and Emotional Learning (CASEL) at the University of Illinois in Chicago, the Centre for Social and Emotional Education (CSEE) at Columbia University, New York, the European Affective Education Network and the National Pastoral Care Association-UK, where Social and Emotional Aspects of Learning (SEAL) are an intrinsic part of the school curriculum. The work emanating from these organizations provides a powerful impetus for schools to focus on the social and emotional aspects of development and learning, alongside traditional academic elements.

The growing interest in social and emotional aspects of development has been stimulated by the popularity of the concept of emotional intelligence. Emotional intelligence, as explored by Salovey and his colleagues (Salovey et al., 1999) and popularized by Daniel Goleman (1998; 2005), has in recent years been acknowledged as an important component of human development.

Emotional intelligence includes self-awareness and impulse control, persistence, zeal, self-motivation, empathy and social expressiveness. Goleman points out that IQ accounts for only 20 per cent of the factors that determine success in life. Likewise, he asserts that academic intelligence has little to do with emotional life. A whole host of factors, including what he describes as emotional intelligence, account for the greater part of an individual's successful transition through life. He points out that there are different ways of being smart and that emotional intelligence is one of them. Emotional intelligence is not fixed at birth but can be nurtured and strengthened. While the brain has no emotional centre, there are several systems or circuits that disperse regulation of a given emotion. Emotional competence consists of two major components: personal competence and social competence (Goleman, 1998);

the former includes self-awareness, self-regulation and motivation and is centred on the individual's self-confidence. . Goleman, in particular, raised awareness and appreciation of the elements of successful adaptation that are not dependent on the traditional notion of IQ, that is, cognitive or rational intelligence. These elements interplay between how people think and feel. They contribute to social and emotional competence and ultimately to success in life.

Thus, the teaching of coping skills for everyday life focuses on children's thinking and feeling skills. It teaches about awareness of self and others and giving young people the resources with which to become socially and emotionally competent. The book introduces the theory of coping and the utility of developing tools to engage with young children through drama, visual arts, language and music-based curricula to enable children to develop the skills they need to cope to the best of their abilities. This book enables practitioners (clinical and educational) to utilize coping tools and coping language as a platform from which to develop the skills to cope.

How to use this book

This book is divided into two parts. Part I, Theory for the Practitioner, is an introduction to a range of theories that relate to positive development and coping in the early years. The six chapters in Part II form the practical or 'how to' part of the book.

The book can be used in a variety of ways and in a range of settings such as the home, nursery, preschool or school, as well as in a clinical setting. No volume on educational ideas can capture the full range of possibilities. Our ideas are not exhaustive, and we encourage you to be creative. All the activities can be undertaken in small or large groups or with individuals.

Each of the chapters in Part II draws on a different discipline of group practice, such as music, drama, dance and drawing. Language development, reflection and interaction are emphasized throughout the book. The chapters can each be used as a stand-alone resources, however, the substantial overlap between them means that the ideas contained in one chapter are often applicable in the other disciplines or settings too. For example, problem solving, which features in Chapter 9, is useful for a range of situations and different settings. Chapter 8, Literacy, Language, Words and Coping, is replete with ideas for teachers and clinicians that are equally valid in a family context. As the reader progresses through the volume he or she should be able to apply the contents of one chapter to the others.

This book provides *Situation Images* and *Coping Images* that can be used as visual tools in any format. In addition, *The Early Years Coping Cards* are a set of visual tools that were developed by two of the authors, Erica Frydenberg and Jan Deans (2011), and are available from the Australian Council for Educational Research (http://shop.acer.edu.au/acer-shop/group/EYC). Alternatively the images provided with this book have been designed to capture a comprehensive range of situations and coping strategies for the 4- to 8-year-old age group.

PART 1
Theory for the Practitioner

Development in the Early Years: Some Important Concepts to Consider

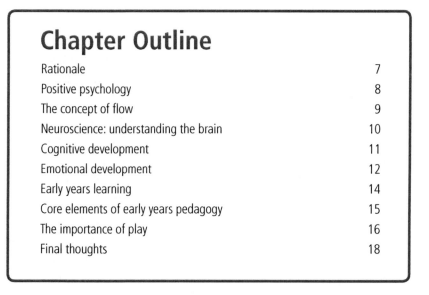

It is important to cope and bounce back because you won't succeed if you scream, cry or get frustrated. In the classroom, you won't understand what you need to do and it can make things worse for you. When I need to cope, I stop. I stop for a bit, take three deep breaths and calm down. I feel happiest when I am watching Funniest Home Videos or playing on my ipod. *Cameron, 8 years*

Rationale

This chapter reviews some key theoretical insights that contribute to an understanding of development and learning in the contemporary context. The positive psychology movement, that in turn has led to the positive education movement, is presented as a backdrop to cognitive and emotional development. Important developments in the neurosciences and early years pedagogy with its emphasis on play are considered.

Positive psychology

Positive psychology is an umbrella term, which captures the shift in psychology research and practice from a deficit model of human development and adaptation to one of capacity and potential. It is underscored by the principle that well-being, happiness and optimal functioning are important endeavours in psychological research and practice. Interest in this positive approach has burgeoned since Martin Seligman and Mihayli Csikszentmihalyi (2000) introduced it at the turn of the twenty-first century and it has inspired educators to pursue the strengths and virtues approach in human behaviour and education. This shift is related to efforts to focus on how people can flourish in a wide range of settings within the home, the workplace and the community in general. While the movement started with adults, before quickly moving on to the world of adolescents and young adults, its emphasis on the here and now means it has a great deal of relevance and application to the world of young children. Young children in their early years are full of enthusiasm for exploration, enquiry, activity and learning. They are curious and readily engage with activities in the learning environment. It is these positive attributes that should be harnessed, fostered and retained throughout the developmental years to nurture positive affect and minimize and reduce negative affect (Diener, 2000). Young people can be equipped for optimal growth and development by exploring how to deal with situations that might be difficult and emotionally challenging.

There are six factors that have been identified as contributing to psychological well-being: autonomy, personal growth, self-acceptance, purpose in life, environmental mastery and positive relations with others (Ryff and Keyes, 1995). While Keyes (2005) was concerned with the adult world, many of the elements that contribute to well-being are readily applicable to young children. For example, in the early years the six factors might manifest themselves as follows:

Help others

- autonomy – I can do it alone
- personal growth – curiosity and engagement
- self-acceptance – what I did is ok
- purpose in life – I want to do
- environmental mastery – I can do feeling
- positive relations with others – I can help others and others can help me.

The concept of flow

In the context of positive development, the concept of flow has emerged from the study of gifted and highly successful adolescents and adults. However, it also has ready application to younger aged children. Flow is a subjective state that people report when they are completely involved in something to the point of total engrossment. Time may appear to 'stand still' and the activity becomes all-important, such as when one is engrossed in a book, playing sport, having a conversation and so on (Csikszentmihalyi, 1990). It is the depth of involvement that is intrinsically rewarding. Flow usually begins when a person takes on tasks or challenges just above his or her skill level. This leads to complexity, and the individual needs to find new challenges and perfect new skills in order to avoid anxiety. When one performs necessary tasks without conscious effort the sense of time can become distorted. The activity becomes 'auto telic', that is, worth doing for its own sake. In the early years this concept is driven by such things as curiosity or the sheer pleasure of engagement in a task. It occurs because children need the stimulation and challenge of activities both within their developmental capacity as well as stretching beyond into more difficult tasks.

Neuroscience: understanding the brain

In recent years there has been a keen interest in understanding the human brain and its relationship to lifelong learning and how deficits in one part of the brain can be compensated by developments in another. Knowledge of neuroscience is work in progress. But it is understood that brain development continues from infancy through to adulthood.

The human body has a symmetry running from the top of the head to the toes, that is, left arm and right arm and so on. The brain also has two hemispheres, left and right. The right hemisphere generally controls the activities on the left side of the body and is associated with spatial abilities and face recognition. The left hemisphere deals with language, mathematics and logic, and is responsible for activities on the right side of the body. The brain's elements are complex. The hemispheres communicate through a set of up to 250 million fibres called the corpus callosum. There are two lobes in each hemisphere associated with particular functions. The frontal lobe is associated with planning and action, the temporal lobe is important for audition, memory and object recognition, the parietal lobe is involved with sensation and spatial processing and the occipital lobe is essential for vision. A complex set of interconnecting neurons joins each lobe. New neurons continue to generate throughout life. They communicate through interconnections or synapses and these are pruned or strengthened according to how often they are used. The two hemispheres work together for all cognitive tasks. That is, the brain is an integrated functioning system.

There is general consensus today that infants do not start with a *tabula rasa* (a clear slate without knowledge) but they are active learners regardless. Children develop theories about the world around them and the way it works from an early age. These theories are constantly modified. Parts of the brain are primed for language acquisition but this cannot take place without the catalyst of experience.

Emotional regulation is important for a number of social and relational reasons but particularly because anger and distress impede learning. Brain functioning, particularly in the amygdala, releases hormones that influence how information is transmitted along the nervous system. The frontal lobe of the brain is relatively late to mature and that is the most rational part of our cognitions. Adults are expected to control their emotions, but aspects of emotion regulation begin developing though the early years of childhood (Centre for Research and Innovations, 2007). As Bruce Compas (2009) has pointed out, executive functioning continues development through childhood, partly as a result of myelination of the prefrontal areas that lasts throughout an extended period. So, while coping and emotion regulation are an important part of early years' development, they continue to develop as children are required to manage increasingly complex emotions from early childhood through to adulthood.

Cognitive development

Cognition can be defined as the inner processes of the mind that enable knowing and understanding. There are two widely recognized and helpful approaches to understanding cognitive development in children. Jean Piaget's (1970) cognitive developmental stage theory focused on the stages of development through which children progress, while Lev Vygotsky's (1962) socio-cultural theory emphasized the social relational context in which learning occurs. Both have been widely influential in the twentieth century and beyond. The first stage that Piaget identified was the sensory-motor stage during the first two years of life. This is followed by the preoperational stage from 2–7 years. Rapid development of representation takes place during this period but there is limited development in logical thought. It is now known that Piaget underestimated the cognitive competence of preoperational thinkers. The third stage, concrete operations, between ages 7–11 years is represented by thinking that is more logical, flexible and organized. In contrast to Piaget, who focused on the child as an individual learner, Vygotsky focused on the child in the social context, where adults can lead and support.

The implications for the early years are that adults need to be sensitive to children's developmental stages and accepting of individual differences. While development follows a series of orderly and systematic steps, it is continuous but uneven and can vary from one individual to another. In most areas development is a result of both maturation and learning and is cumulative. Children are active partners in their learning, all of which takes place in a context, the classroom, playground or home setting. This is relevant for all domains of learning, whether they relate to language, literacy, numeracy or social and emotional development.

Emotional development

The works of Sigmund Freud (1964) and Erik Erikson (1968; 1985) are important in helping us to understand personality and social and emotional development. Sigmund Freud, founder of the psychoanalytic movement, proposed a theory of psychosexual development that was the first to stress the importance of early experience for later development. Essentially Freud proposed a number of stages through which the individual confronts a series of conflicts between biological drives and social expectations. For Freud, the way parents manage children's sexual and aggressive drives in the early years determines psychological adjustment. He believed that the id is the part of the personality responsible for biological needs and desires. The ego is the rational part of the personality, which reconciles the demands of the id, the external world and the conscience. The third component is the superego, the seat of conscience, which is often in conflict with the id. Freud's theory is often criticized for its extensive emphasis on psychosexual development but the notion of conscience and superego, which develops initially between the ages of 3–6 and continues through the latency years between 6–11, is highly relevant in terms of psychosocial development, particularly as it relates to empathy. Empathy evolves as part of the development of the superego.

Erik Erikson, one of Freud's followers, expanded the psychosexual framework to focus on psychosocial outcomes. Erikson considered each period of development, from infancy through to old age. Starting with birth and infancy, which are reflected in notions of 'trust and mistrust', children move to the first three years, notable for the development of autonomy, shame and doubt. Beyond, the ages 3–6 are marked by the idea of initiative versus guilt. This stage is distinguished by attempts at independence, as the child endeavours to become more assertive. It is also about a willingness to begin new activities and explore new directions. The fourth stage, the one most relevant for the early years (6–11), is, according to Erikson, exemplified by industry versus inferiority. Erikson's strict categorizations have also been criticized. Nevertheless they remain useful markers in recognizing the importance of initiative and a sense of purpose and ambition from an early age, followed by an eagerness for industry, and to work and cooperate with others.

Humans are born with the ability to express six basic emotions, namely, fear, anger, sadness, joy, surprise and disgust. These have been termed primary emotions. Secondary emotions develop from 2 years of age and they help children to evaluate their own behaviour and that of others. These emotions include self-consciousness, including shame, embarrassment, guilt, envy and pride. These have been called the social emotions because they are seen as impacting on self-concept. As children approach 2 years of age they are able to understand themselves and they start displaying empathy and a recognition of the feelings of others.

Overall emotional competence is about having well-developed emotional understandings and skills. It is about understanding one's own emotions and those of others. It is also about the capacity to cope with negative emotions, often termed self-regulation.

Positive social experiences play a role in the development of emotion regulation, which in turn can impact a child's ability to cope with stress and develop behavioural control (Wilmshurst, 2008). As children grow and gain more social experience and cognitive sophistication, the social and emotional pattern set in early childhood continues to be refined.

Early years learning

Throughout the Western world there are many publications outlining and detailing both the context and the content of children's learning in the early years. While this book deals primarily with an age range of between 4 and 8, there are elements that are universal. For example, there is significant brain development during the early years that helps us to understand the biological underpinnings and representations of the development of 4–8 year olds. In the context of the early years, play is an important tool to advance both cognitive and emotional development, particularly where relationships are concerned. Our emphasis in this volume is to bring together theory and practice to facilitate optimal growth in children in the context of their schooling and family relationships. Much of what is presented in this book applies to both school and family life. The ideas, which have been trialled in clinical and educational contexts, can also be adapted to children who may have developmental delays that are emotional, cognitive and/or physical. Age is not as important as a child's developmental milestones. Even within the larger group context there may be a need to make adjustments for an individual child or small groups of children.

Age-appropriate learning is achieved in different ways in a structured educational setting. For example, in the preschool years children acquire a range of skills necessary for learning, such as curiosity, cooperation, confidence, creativity, commitment, enthusiasm, persistence, imagination and reflexivity. They develop skills such as problem solving, experimentation, hypothesizing and investigating. They can transfer what they have learned from one setting to another and often resource their learning by connecting with people and technologies. These capacities are demonstrated in different ways at different developmental stages between the ages of 4 and 8 (see Victorian Early Years Learning and Development Framework, 2009, p. 26). Before the age of 5, for instance, a child playing with a globe of the earth might simply wonder, explore and play with the object. By the age of 5 he or she could be questioning and probing for information about the different countries. By 7 the child may be able to reflect upon and consider the earth and its place in the universe.

Core elements of early years pedagogy

It is widely acknowledged that children's learning is dynamic, complex and holistic and that physical, social, emotional, personal, spiritual, creative, cognitive and linguistic aspects of learning are all intricately interwoven and interrelated (Commonwealth of Australia, 2009). In the learning context it is desirable that children recognize their capacity to learn and develop and have an impact on others. In order to achieve this, children's learning needs to be scaffolded to go to the next stage. That is, in the school or family context, it is about building on children's existing knowledge and skills to facilitate learning. This is true for all facets of education, whether it is the curriculum as it relates to language and literacy, or the aspects of classroom practice that focus on social and emotional learning. Thus, classroom enquiry and facilitated activities take the child to the next stage of cognitive understanding and skill acquisition. Children demonstrate their learning and understandings in different ways and learn through different modes of activity. The early years' situation and coping images enable the user to talk about coping in a variety of contexts and ways, such as through language, literacy, art, drama, music and child-directed play. Each area of activity enables the language of coping to be reinforced and provides the opportunity for children who learn in diverse ways to be engaged and their interest maintained in the social and emotional aspect of pedagogy. The children's voices become an intrinsic part of the activity. This can be achieved through intentional teaching or play-based learning.

Through the learning experience, it is expected that children will develop a strong sense of identity. They will take on a sense of well-being and become confident and involved learners and effective communicators. These outcomes can be achieved through the normal course of school experience. Through the give and take of conversation and collaborative classroom practice, children will be able to demonstrate an increased capacity to cooperate and work with others. They will learn about emotions and learn to be aware of their own emotions and those of others. Moreover, they will be able to respect diversity and gradually learn to read the behaviour of others and respond appropriately.

There is a general consensus in all curricula documents that educators need to engage with the family, and in that sense when it comes to talking about coping, it is helpful to brief parents as to what is being done and to help them adopt some of the language and strategies that are used in the school setting. These can be reinforced in the home through modelling and social learning.

Equity and diversity are very much at the forefront of education today. Children are keen observers and quickly assess the ways in which adults interact with each other and with them. When it comes to diversity and culture, there is theoretically an infinite range of cultural settings that children may find themselves in. They bring these experiences into the school settings, adding to the richness of classroom practice.

Reflective practice is another important area in education. Ideally young children are thoughtful about their responses to situations and to reflect on their own actions. That is, able to review outcomes in a helpful and self-analytical way. Coping research reveals, for example, that it is not only one's actions that are important but how they impact on others that determine outcomes. At the same time a belief in one's own capacity is also important.

The importance of play

Fantasy and imaginative play are significant features of early years' development. While the nature of play changes dramatically between four and eight years, the shift is more from parallel play to cooperative play, where others are involved, there are leaders and followers, and there is communication between players. Sometimes the others are just imaginary friends. Generally speaking, play is to children as work is to adults. It is the discovery of the self and the other; the discovery of real time and space. There is both a simultaneous dependency and a movement towards individuation and separation. During this process a transition object such as a security blanket or toy often helps the

Saying sorry

child to separate from the critical other, usually a parent or a significant caregiver.

Play is essentially a form of communication and with the child's permission adults can enter their fantasy world. They can join in, listen and observe what is being communicated. Play has been described as the 'royal road to the unconscious' in that it can give us insights into anxieties and concerns (Neven, 1996). There is a place for directive play, such as utilizing toys that might represent a visit to the doctor or moving to a new school. Non-directive or free play involves children choosing the objects or toys and setting the situations themselves. In either form of play the adult needs to be a non-judgemental observer/participant. Play can be used for rehearsal and it can also be used for healing. It can be used as a safe way of expressing frustration and anger, behind a puppet or a doll, for example. All children want to be heard and sometimes the safe haven of play allows their fears and wishes to be noted. The situation and coping images can therefore be used in a range of contexts for direct or indirect instruction or through enabling coping focused play to occur.

Final thoughts

Taking account of age and stage of development, culture, context and situation, enables us to use tools in a range of settings, particularly in school, family and clinical contexts to deal with a range of children's concerns. Thus enabling them to continue on the path of healthy development so that they can thrive and deal with a host of issues that they are likely to meet in their journey through childhood.

Stress, Concerns and Coping: The Worries of Young Children

When my rabbit, Nudge, got myxomatosis it was sad to know he was going to die. I took lots of photos so that I could remember him. I will always remember his soft white fur. I might make an album of his photos. *Mika, 7 years*

Rationale

Children experience stress early in life and the way they appraise situations and cope accordingly is based on prior experience, parental influences and social and emotional development. Coping skills are an intrinsic resource but equally important are the extrinsic resources and supports that are available to children throughout their lives. An understanding of the way children cope with daily stressors and concerns can help educational professionals, parents and clinicians to better support their healthy cognitive and social and emotional development, as well as the environmental factors that provide opportunities for young children to thrive rather than simply endure life's ups and downs.

Setting the scene

It is now well established that children, like adults, experience stress. While unsettling events can be concerning and worrisome in themselves, it is the magnitude of the resulting responses that is most crucial. Constant stress can be corrosive and take a heavy toll on the body and its immune system. It can lead to a range of conditions such as headaches, stomach aches and eczema. Prolonged stress can also be deleterious to brain function (Hampton, 2006). Stress affects the regions of the brain that are responsible for executive functioning, emotion regulation

Scream/tantrum

and resistance to distraction. Children with better executive functioning cope more successfully with stress.

All children can experience stress, but how they respond to it is dependent on age and their associated cognitive and social and emotional development, temperament and environmental factors. Children's stresses may appear insignificant to adults but, because children have less experience and a limited coping repertoire, even small changes can have a huge impact on their feelings of safety and security. Early experiences and adversity may also influence a child's view of the world. It is also thought that fear is most prevalent in children between the ages of 2 and 6 (Papalia and Olds, 1989) and that girls tend to express more fears than boys (Bauer, 1976). While studies have shown that children as young as 5 are able to articulate worries, the nature of cognitive thought processes becomes more complex with maturity (Wilmshurst, 2008). For example, children from 8 years of age tend to worry about psychological well-being and social approval (Vasey, 1993).

According to Youngs (1985), children experience two main kinds of stress:

1. normative or developmental stress, which occurs as part of the growing experience, and
2. life-change stress such as an illness, injury or death of a loved one.

Youngs (1985) identified the common sources of stress in young children as they progress through school. These stressors are reflected in order of their intensity in the following table.

Stressors of young children

Stressor	Signs/Manifestation of Stress
4–6 years old	
Feeling of uncertainty and fear of being abandoned by a significant adult.	There may be references to this fear in naptimes and sleep; daydreaming; crying in the absence of parents; nail-biting.
Fear of wetting themselves.	Makes frequent trips to bathroom; wets him or herself occasionally; may exhibit nail-biting; thumb-sucking. Some children may not ask to go to the bathroom because they do not know how to ask to excuse themselves.

Fear of being reprimanded or punished by teachers.	Has the desire to please the teacher but may not know how to do so, and fears that the teacher may not be pleased or may even be angry; afraid of expressing disapproval of teachers because of fear of teachers' reactions.

6–7 years old

Fear of taking the bus.	Asks parents to drive him/her to school.
Fear of wetting in class.	Is overly concerned about the possibility of wetting himself; spends much time thinking about the consequences; daydreams and occasionally wets in class due to anxiety.
Teacher disapproval.	Continual seeking teacher's approval as opposed to more independent action.
Being ridiculed by peers and older students in the school setting.	Turns 'inward' and expresses desire not to attend school.
Receiving first report card and not passing to second grade.	Uses 'negative self-talk', and exhibits low self-esteem.

7–8 years old

Frequently misses a particular parent.	Desires to return home and be with parent.
Fear of not being able to understand a given lesson (e.g. won't be able to pass a test).	Is inattentive, cries and impatient with self.
Not being selected to be a 'teacher helper' or not getting attention from teacher.	Feels disliked by teacher; seeks any teacher attention (positive or negative).
Fear of being disciplined by the teacher.	Avoids direct eye contact in a teacher–student activity.
Fear of being different from other children in dress and appearance.	Feels disliked by other children.

Worries can become stresses when the worry is intense and or persistent.

What is coping?

Stress and coping is one of the most highly researched areas in the field of psychology. Stress can be construed as the mismatch between the demands of a situation and a person's perceived capacity to cope. That is, stress occurs when one does not feel that he or she has the resources to cope. For this reason the research relating to stress has generally focused on incapacity and lack of well-being. In recent years the focus of interest has shifted from exploring stress and the demands that circumstances place on individuals to studying capacity and achievement, that is, how people cope.

Coping comprises our thoughts, feelings and actions in response to the demands of a situation. The way people respond to situations affects their health, well-being and even, ultimately, their success in life. There are many facets to coping. People may react to a situation in many different ways; some of which may be helpful and some not. Outcomes do matter and the way one learns to assess situations, deal with them and reflect on outcomes is all-important.

Richard Lazarus is responsible for the seminal work in the field of coping, at the Stress and Coping laboratory in Berkeley, California. He described coping as a transaction between a person and the environment, represented as 'constantly changing cognitive and behavioural efforts to manage specific external and/or internal demands that are appraised as taxing or exceeding the resources of the person' (Lazarus and Folkman, 1984, p. 141). The key concept that this frequently cited definition highlights is that both a situation and a person's response to it can change throughout the course of the transaction. Coping is a dynamic and ongoing phenomenon which should not be measured in the same way as inherent traits or capacities. Appraisal or judgement of a situation is an important aspect of the coping process. Whether a situation is appraised as one of threat, harm, loss or challenge determines the outcome.

Building on this model, the coping process can be construed as a continuous, circular process, set in motion by a specific situation. First there is the appraisal of the situation, followed by the determination of whether one has the capacity to deal with it. Then follows the question of how one accesses resources to assist in dealing with the situation and, finally, the coping or management. The outcome is then assessed to determine whether the action was effective and whether it can become part of the individual's coping repertoire (see Frydenberg, 2008). Skinner and Zimmer-Gembeck (2007) have extended these models in their multi-level adaptation to highlight the developmental perspective. This factors in a time-specific and developmental aspect, which recognizes that at each level there is growing sophistication in the coping process.

Appraisal

The concept of appraisal is one of the basic tenets of coping theory and the first step in the coping process. Cognitive appraisal is what a person does to evaluate whether a particular encounter is relevant to his or her well-being. In each encounter two forms of appraisal are said to take place: *primary appraisal*, where the question 'What is at stake in terms of potential harm or benefit?' is asked, and *secondary appraisal*, which deals with the question 'What can be done about the situation or what are the options or resources available?' The appraisals may initiate a chain of activity and coping actions to manage a situation.

Appraisal is associated with both the type and amount of coping. Different stressors may be at play depending on whether a situation takes place in the home or at school, for instance. Stress at home might be related to interactions with siblings, for example, while at school it might involve tasks that the child is required to complete. Findings

Afraid of trying something new

based on older children hold true even for younger ones. Nine- and ten-year-old children reported harmful or loss-inducing situations as the most stressful. When asked to describe a stressful event children spontaneously described a situation that could cause them harm.

The organization of coping

In an attempt to organize the numerous ways in which people cope, efforts have been made to categorize and group coping actions under labels, such as 'ways of coping' (Lazarus and Folkman, 1984,) 'coping families' (Skinner et al., 2003) or 'coping strategies' (Frydenberg and Lewis, 1993). Lazarus and Folkman (1984) group their coping strategies under two main categories: 'problem-focused' and 'emotion-focused'. The former deals with the problem, while emotion-focused strategies are used when an individual deems a situation to be out of his or her sphere of control. This generally leads to non-productive strategies such as self-blame or worrying.

Other dichotomous groupings include 'engaging and disengaging coping' (Tobin et al., 1989), 'approach and avoidance coping' (Ebata and Moos, 1991) and 'active and passive coping' (Denham and Burton, 2003). Each of these groupings generally sees stressors as either controllable or outside the purview of an individual's influence. There have been attempts to consider tripartite groupings, such as that of Amirkhan (1990) who proposed problem solving, support seeking and avoidance. Frydenberg and Lewis (1993) also conceptualized three styles of coping, based on an Australian study of nearly 650 adolescents.

The first of these is 'productive coping', which generally involves productive means of approaching a problem. The second 'non-productive strategies', is a largely unhelpful way of dealing with stress. Both of these styles involve problem solving and emotion-focused means of coping. This contrasts with the idea that maladaptive outcomes can only be linked to emotion-focused coping; indeed emotion-based information used to guide thoughts and actions is now deemed critically important (Frydenberg, 2008). The third way of dealing with stress is known as 'relational coping'. In this style of coping an individual turns to other networks of support, be they familial, social, spiritual or professional (Frydenberg and Lewis, 1993). Each of these categories contains a number of coping strategies. There is no agreement on the number of these strategies among researchers and they vary from Folkman and Lazarus' (1985) eight coping scales (one problem-focused and seven emotion-focused) to Frydenberg and Lewis's eighteen coping strategies (1993). Regardless of how it is categorized, coping is affected both by developmental level and personal history, that is, previous experiences of success or failure.

Coping and emotions

The relationship between coping and emotions is important as emotions are generally believed to interfere with cognition and coping. They often appear to dominate, leaving the individual floundering in a confusion of feelings and responses. Historically, coping has been viewed as a response to emotion. In recent years, there has been a shift in perspective to a point where the two are understood to be in a reciprocal, dynamic relationship. Just as emotion determines how an encounter is evaluated, so the outcome determines the individual's emotional state, both in the ongoing interaction and in future interactions. Folkman and Lazarus (1988) distinguish this both from the Darwinian approach, where emotions such as fear and anger are thought to come to the aid of the organism in the face of threat, and also from the ego-psychological approach, which involves reference to cognitive processes such as denial, repression, suppression, intellectualization and problem solving in an effort to reduce stress and anxiety. Although there is no readily agreed definition of emotion, there is general agreement that emotions comprise an experiential (affect, appraisal), physiological and behavioural (action for readiness) component (Izard, 1993; Frijda, 1993) and that these are expressed through separate systems such as the verbal reporting of feelings, overt behaviour and expressive physiology. The metaphorical language of negative emotions generally portrays them as an irresistible force. Thus much of the emotion-focused conceptualization of coping in the literature has focused on the maladaptive.

A more recent perspective of emotion has focused on its adaptive nature and ways in which individuals can organize social communication, goal achievement and cognitive processes from an early age (Izard,

Stop and think

1993; Pekrun et al., 2002). This view sees emotions as a major organizing force with interpersonal and intrapersonal regulatory effects. Three theoretical constructs exemplify a functionalist view of emotion in personality research: emotional competence (Saarni, 1990), emotional intelligence (Salovey and Mayer, 1990) and emotional creativity (Averill and Thomas-Knowles, 1991). All contribute to healthy interpersonal and intrapersonal functioning. Emotional competence is essentially self-efficacy in the context of 'emotion-eliciting social transactions' (Saarni, 1990). The concept of emotional intelligence has integrated the literature from multiple intelligences (Gardner, 1983) and can be construed as a subset of social intelligence. Emotional creativity involves the creation of novel emotions. Overall, all three constructs are highly relevant to identifying and regulating one's own emotions, as well as reading and responding to the emotions of others in an effort to achieve the best outcomes.

Individuals differ in how they perceive, express, understand and manage emotional phenomena. Essentially, emotional intelligence is the ability to both monitor one's own and others' feelings and emotions, as well as to regulate and use emotion-based information to guide thinking and action. In contrast, traditional intelligence is considered to deal with reasoning and analytical abilities.

A child's perspective

The way children conceive emotions indicates that they tend to see the possibility for change as originating from the situation itself, rather than from internal or mental sources (Carroll and Steward, 1984; Harris and Olthof, 1982). They are also relatively facile with regard to more situation- or problem-based approaches, particularly when controllable stressors are involved (Band and Weisz, 1988). During the preschool years, children also become progressively able to control their emotions and tolerate frustration. Young children at the age of 4 increasingly behave in a way that balances personal goals with the goals of others as their cognitive and language skills mature (Kopp, 2009).

Some studies have shown that young children tend to seek support from adults and withdraw or engage in behavioural activities as a form of distraction in their coping repertoire (Hampel and Petermann, 2005; Skinner and Zimmer-Gembeck, 2007). It has been posited that the use of emotion-focused coping begins to develop during early childhood and that preschoolers have an emergent capacity to utilize strategic emotion-focused coping (Kopp, 2009). When coping is examined across the life span, a significant change occurs at preschool age, marking a noticeable shift from interpersonal co-regulation to intrapersonal self-regulation (Compas, 2009). Past research has also shown that coping strategies become more stressor specific with age (Fields and Prinz, 1997). Young children may have fewer coping skills and therefore have less flexibility in selecting and utilizing coping strategies (Pincus and Friedman, 2004).

A theoretical model of coping

The model of coping that best reflects the research posits that coping is a function of situational determinants and an individual's characteristics, perception of the situation and coping intentions. The individual brings a host of biological dispositional, personal and family history and family climate characteristics. It is how these impact on the individual's perception of the situation that is of interest. Following an appraisal of the situation, the individual assesses the likely impact of the stress, that is, whether the consequences are likely to lead to 'loss', 'harm' 'threat' or 'challenge', and what resources (personal or interpersonal) are available to the individual to deal with the situation. The intent of the action, along with the action itself, determines the outcome. Following a response, the outcome is reviewed or reappraised (*tertiary appraisal* or *reappraisal*) and another response may follow. There may be a subsequent development in an individual's coping repertoire. The circular nature of the process illustrates that strategies are likely to be tried again or rejected from future use, consequent on the coping experience of the individual.

If the encounter is amenable to change, problem-focused strategies are frequently used. Where the situation is assessed as unchangeable, emotion-focused strategies are more likely to be used (Folkman and Lazarus, 1980). For example, males tend to appraise 'hassles' in terms of a challenge and employ problem-focused strategies, whereas females are more inclined to appraise situations as threatening or harmful and use emotion-focused coping (Ptacek et al., 1992).

As stated above, whether or not a stressor is controllable is an important factor in coping. A study by Compas and colleagues (1988) found that academic stressors were assessed as more controllable than interpersonal stressors; problem-focused strategies were generally used more often than emotion-focused strategies to deal with the academic stressors. It was also found that a low perceived control of the stressor resulted in greater use of emotion-focused coping, whereas problem-focused coping was more likely to be employed in situations of high perceived control. Another interesting finding was that where self-reports and maternal reports indicated that emotional or behavioural problems existed, there was a higher usage of emotion-focused coping. On the other hand, where there were no emotional or behavioural problems, there was a higher usage of problem-focused coping.

Lazarus emphasizes the central role of cognitions in emotional outcomes, asserting that when people experience situations as a 'hassle', it is the meaning that they give to a transaction, and whether they appraise the situation as threatening, harmful or challenging that may have an impact on the emotion generated and the coping reaction (Folkman et al., 1987). This is what is meant by the 'perception of the situation'.

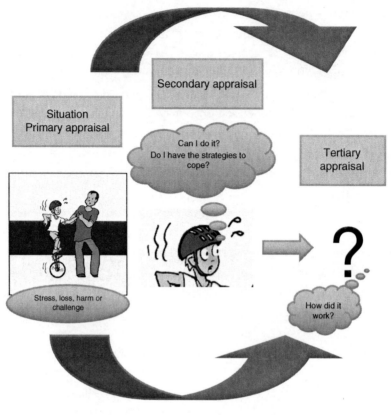

Coping model

Psychological stress resides neither in the person nor in the situation, but depends on the transaction between the two, that is, how the person appraises the event and how he or she adapts to it. Thus for some young people, being singled out to talk in front of the class may be stressful, while to others it is perceived as part of the excitement of school. Ultimately, coping describes how people 'mobilize, modulate, manage and co-ordinate their behaviour and emotions (or fail to do so) under stress' (Skinner and Zimmer-Gembeck, 2009, p. 6.). These researchers also point out the importance of being developmentally sensitive.

The coping figure presented above indicates how when we are confronted with a situation, such as trying out something difficult or new, the question is asked, 'Can I do it?' or 'Do I have the strategies to cope?' and depending on the outcome whether the child or person learns from the experience. If the experience and outcome are positive, they are more likely to make an attempt on another occasion.

What we know about coping

Research has found that coping strategies which focus on problem solving and positive cognitions are related to fewer emotional, behavioural and substance use problems (Compas et al., 1988; Ebata and Moos, 1991). In contrast, avoidant or non-productive coping is generally associated with poor adaptation and more mental health problems in adolescents (Ebata and Moos, 1991; Frydenberg and Lewis, 1999; Sandler et al., 1997). Most researchers have reported gender differences in coping showing that girls tend to turn to their peers while boys are more likely to keep to themselves, particularly when they are most stressed. In the early years it may be that boys are more likely to act up and be aggressive rather than withdrawn.

Cross-cultural studies show clear differences between communities that are culturally diverse, such as those of Australia and Colombia, and a greater number of similarities between young people from more homogenous communities such as those in Germany and Ireland (Frydenberg et al., 2003). There are clear indications that coping is unique to each culture and context. While theoretical insights can be gained from one setting which may transfer to another, it is important to consider coping in each context. What are the skills required and what works? Young people who have greater access to resources such as family support and success in learning are likely to cope more productively. The implication of this is that young people need to be skilled in coping and attention paid to the resources that are available to them. There are age and developmental differences in coping which need to be considered. Individuals cope with different situations at different stages of their development and both cognitive and emotional development need to be taken into account. Nevertheless, children are highly aware of how others, both peers and adults, around them cope. Social learning and modelling are important teaching tools.

Coping and the early years

It is clear that children experience stress from an early age. They are likely to appraise a situation as one of threat, harm, loss or challenge and cope accordingly. They draw on previous experience and can reflect on or appraise outcomes. There are developmental and situational differences with regard to what children have to deal with and how they cope. Coping skills are an important part of their internal resource base, as are the external resources and supports available to them.

How we can teach coping?

This question could be reframed to ask, 'When is it too early to talk about coping and to teach coping skills?' In the 1990s, tools were developed in the Australian context to measure coping. Two of these, the Adolescent Coping Scale and the Coping Scale for Adults (Frydenberg and Lewis, 1993, 1997) have proved useful in identifying constructs that are applicable to children, adolescents and adults and over time these have been used for developing coping skills. These instruments led to the development of programmes such as *Best of Coping* (Frydenberg and Brandon, 2007a, 2007b), the CD-Rom *Coping for Success* (Frydenberg, 2007) and more recently, *Think Positively: A Course for Developing Coping Skills in Adolescence* (Frydenberg, 2010; Frydenberg and Deans, 2011). For several years theory and our understanding of coping skills have been used to develop early years coping tools for 4–8 year olds. These tools have been used to explore young children's coping and to provide insights into the applications reported in this volume.

Coping and social and emotional competence

Several theorists have argued that emotions underlie the development of problem-solving ability, behavioural adjustment, social interactions and relationships and moral behaviour (Eisenberg and Fabes, 1998; Izard, 2002). Specifically, social and emotional competence and coping have been identified as protective factors for children against emotional and behavioural problems (Denham, 2006; Blechman et al., 1995). Social and emotional competence has been described as comprising emotional expressiveness, emotion knowledge, regulation of emotion and behaviour, social problem-solving and social and relationship skills (Denham, 2006).

Theorists of coping also discuss the regulation of emotion and emotion-related behaviours. Lazarus and Folkman (1984) defined coping as cognitive and behavioural efforts to manage specific external or internal demands that are appraised as exceeding the resources of the individual. Eisenberg and colleagues defined coping as a subset of the broader category of self-regulation in response to stress (Eisenberg et al., 1997). They further distinguished between three aspects of self-regulation: 'attempts to directly regulate emotion' (e.g. emotion-focused coping), 'attempts to regulate the situation' (e.g. problem-focused coping) and 'attempts to regulate emotionally driven behaviour (e.g. behaviour regulation)' (Eisenberg et al., 1997, p. 45). They argued that coping is not always conscious and intentional (Eisenberg et al., 1997) and thus includes both volitional and automatic responses to stress. Hence, coping includes regulating one's internal emotional arousal and behaviour in response to the stressor, as well as the regulation of the source of emotional arousal (Liew et al., 2003). Behavioural and emotion regulation have been found to be central to school learning and success (Raver, 2002; Zins et al., 2004).

Assessing coping competencies in early years

Susanne Denham, one of the leading investigators in the area of social and emotional competence in preschool-aged children, argued for the importance of social and emotional competence for school readiness and the availability of appropriate measures of social and emotional competence (Denham, 2006). Similarly, despite the compelling empirical link between coping and social and academic success, measuring coping has been fraught with difficulty, partly due to the lack of both definitional and methodological agreements among investigators. In a review of studies on coping in childhood and adolescence, the authors argued that many of the problems in the field come from the lack of clarity and consensus regarding the nature of coping during childhood and adolescence and the limitations in measures of coping available for these development periods (Compas et al., 2001).

Behavioural reports from adult informants (e.g. parents and teachers) are usually used in studies of early childhood coping, although young children's self-reports might be cross-referenced with adult observations. The studies described in the next chapter represent recent efforts at conceptualizing and measuring coping in the early years.

Final thoughts

There is clear evidence to suggest that young Australian children (age 4 and older) are capable of using coping strategies to regulate their emotions or behaviours and report using a range of coping actions. Forty-six 4-year-old preschoolers were asked to describe how they would cope with seven typical situations experienced by preschoolers. It was discovered that preschoolers can articulate coping strategies that could then be categorized as either productive or non-productive coping. This three-phase investigation is reported in detail in Chapter 3.

Situations and Coping Strategies: An Introduction to Coping Images

Sometimes in life you have to deal with something you don't like or have to live with something really tricky. Coping is about being resilient. You keep going and do your best. *Thomas, 8 years*

Rationale

Coping images stimulate conversations and learning opportunities on a range of everyday issues that have been identified as challenging and stressful for children between the ages of 4–8 years. The purpose of the images is to help educators, parents and clinicians support children in talking about what is important to them and how they feel about situations that are difficult to manage. The idea is to create a shared language of coping, moving children from a simplistic or superficial level to one that is deeper and more complex.

Setting the scene

Despite technological advances and the lifestyle benefits that accrue from progress, depression and other mental health issues are being experienced in epidemic proportions in many Western communities, and in particular among young people and children. The search for effective ways to reverse this trend has resulted in a significant shift in psychological approach, from a focus on helplessness and pathology to a more positive orientation that emphasizes health and well-being. The fostering of personal agency is an important component in inoculating children, young people and adults against depression and freeing them to achieve success. An emphasis on coping rather than on stress and distress is a feature of this positive orientation. It is helpful to construe coping as a continuum that extends from the management of stress and adaptation to achieving success and flourishing in the pursuit of goals and meeting the challenges of everyday life. What is clear is that the earlier these skills are developed the better.

There is overwhelming agreement that social and emotional development is critical for the success and well-being of young children. Emphasis in the early years of schooling is placed on enabling children to develop a strong sense of identity and well-being, as well as becoming confident and involved learners and effective communicators. In addition, it is considered important for children to be able to demonstrate an increased capacity to cooperate and work with others, to self-regulate and gradually learn to read the behaviour of others and respond appropriately. The ultimate aim is to promote in children a strong sense of self and to help them to develop a range of the social and emotional skills that are seen as essential precursors for successful learning.

It is widely understood by educational professionals, parents and clinicians that the development of social and emotional competence contributes to a young child's success within the preschool environment and has a major influence on the establishment of positive peer relationships. Such competence is also considered very important in relation to school readiness and has implications for the way people cope with daily stressors throughout our lives. (Aldwin et al., 2010).

From theory to practice

For many years, educational professionals have identified the value of extending theoretical insights about young children's coping to the early years to develop a greater understanding of which situations concern young children most and what are the age and situation-appropriate coping strategies that children employ in the early years. In order to achieve this, the authors engaged in a three-phase process. Phase 1 was designed to establish a foundation from which a measure could be developed by identifying preschool children's coping responses and matching them with parents' understandings of these responses. Phase 2 involved the development of a nomenclature of coping responses for preschool children, including the development of visual representations of challenging situations which were used to stimulate children's verbal responses about their coping strategies. In Phase 3 the authors explored the utilization of coping situations and responses in multiple settings and across multiple aspects of the curriculum, such as in drama, visual arts, language, music and in clinical settings where children are focused on developing skills to deal with particularly stressful circumstances.

Losing something or someone special

Exploring coping in young children

When it comes to assessing children's coping behaviour, studies generally use behavioural reports from adult informants (e.g. parents and teachers). It is also possible to cross-reference young children's self-reports with adult observations. The studies that the authors undertook to measure children's coping utilized children's self-reports as well as those of their parents and teachers.

In a study by Deans and colleagues (2010), which employed a qualitative research methodology, 4- to 5-year-old inner-city Australian children were interviewed and found to spontaneously report more coping strategies than those recognized and reported by parents. When children's coping strategies were considered together with those of their parents, the children reported the use of more 'active coping' strategies (e.g. 'I take care of myself') and fewer 'passive coping' strategies (e.g. 'I would feel sad') than those identified in the children by their parents. The researchers suggested that this could be because some coping strategies are not within the range of the children's awareness. Another explanation is that young children are generally disinclined to talk about strategies that are perceived to be negative. The study showed that parent and child reports of 'relational coping' strategies were similar. The young children's spontaneity in describing how they cope with challenging situations points to their capacity to articulate their understandings of coping and reinforces the viability of assessing social and emotional coping competencies in the early years.

The first phase made it clear that Australian 4-year-old children are capable of using coping strategies to regulate their emotions or behaviours and to report a range of coping strategies. In Phase 2, Chalmers (2010) interviewed preschoolers in an early learning centre to elicit their coping strategies when dealing with challenging situations appropriate to a 7 year old. The authors categorized the coping responses into productive and non-productive coping styles, based on Frydenberg's (1993) classification of coping. The results showed that 76 per cent of the children reported the use of no more than one non-productive coping strategy across the set situations. The majority of them (74 per cent) had a repertoire of productive strategies that they could apply to at least five or six different situations. Specifically, the preschoolers most commonly cited problem solving as the coping strategy to use in situations that involved issues of friendship, choices and teasing. This can partly be understood in light of the degree of controllability perceived by the children in these scenarios. When the situation was perceived to be within their control, the children used approach strategies such as problem solving to cope, whereas an uncontrollable stressor is more likely to be handled by avoidance strategies (Band and Weisz, 1988; Hubert et al., 1988). This is consistent with the literature on the distinction between controllable and uncontrollable stressors. In addition, the 4 year olds in the study demonstrated emergent skills in using secondary control strategies such as self-calming and positive self-talk as well as evaluating the efficiency of their coping efforts. The research raises concerns about the substantial proportion of young children (20 per cent–75 per cent) who are not dealing with separation anxiety and teacher and peer issues in a productive manner and would benefit from being taught more efficacious coping strategies.

Coping categories

Extending this preliminary investigation that examined the consistency between children's and their parents' understanding and reporting of coping strategies, Tsurutani (2009) explored parents' and teachers' reports of 4-year-old children's coping behaviours. The nature of preschoolers' coping as reported by parents revealed four dimensions: non-productive (reference to others), non-productive (self-reliant), productive (reference to others) and productive (self-reliant). It was argued that the distinction between self-reliant coping and that which involved reference to others reflected the developmental–transitional stage of the preschoolers who were just beginning to exert greater independence and engage in voluntary responses to stressors after the initial period of reliance on caregivers' coping actions (Skinner and Zimmer-Gembeck, 2007). In contrast, teacher reports of preschoolers' coping were less clearly categorized into self-reliant or reference to others. The coping dimensions reflected one grouping of productive coping and three groupings of non-productive coping: anger, social withdrawal and inhibition. These non-productive coping strategies may indicate a tendency among teachers to be aware of and report strategies as a result of being trained to understand behaviours from an educational and developmental perspective. Furthermore, differences were noted in teachers' and parents' reports in the seek support, do nothing and keep feelings to self coping strategies. These differences could be due to the opportunities offered by the contexts and might indicate the regulatory processes and types of coping strategies encouraged by teachers. While the author acknowledged the exploratory nature of the study, the differences in coping dimensions reported by teachers and parents indicates a variability across informants when documenting young children's coping behaviours. These findings were thought to have implications on the way adaptive coping skills can be fostered and taught to young children.

The development of coping images

It is always helpful to relate coping to a particular situation and this is even more applicable in the early years. Asking a young child to reflect on how he or she deals with a particular situation, rather than in general terms, is essential. For the purpose of this book, and based on previous research, professionally drawn situation and coping images have been provided for readers to use. The reader can create a set of situation and coping images by downloading the colour images from the website.

The images are based on common fearful or challenging situations, such as the fear of separation; fear the dark; fear being teased; fear of negative evaluation by an adult and feeling excluded (Fields and Prinz, 1997; Sorin, 2005). The situation images used for the purpose of this book are the following nine situations identified as most relevant:

- Worrying about leaving someone you love

- Fear of the dark

- Being in trouble with a teacher or parent

- Being bullied or teased

- Losing something or someone special

- Afraid of trying something new

- Wanting to belong to a group

- Getting hurt

- Having a broken toy

The coping actions are as follows:

- Think happy thoughts

- Help others

- Hide

- Hug a toy

- Cry

- Blame others

- Help others/share

- Blame self

- Scream/cry/tantrum

- Blame self/get angry

- Talk to an adult/someone

- Work hard

- Keep feelings to self/stay quiet

- Complain of pain

- Play

- Runaway

- Say sorry

- Stop and think

- Worry (2 versions)

- Stay calm/quiet

- Run away

Final thoughts

Both educational professionals and parents alike report that the cards provide an effective way to help them create and continue conversations with young children. They have also reported that the cards can be used within the family for a wide range of challenging or stressful situations that are confronted on a daily basis. They can be used by parents, professionals and teachers to develop a deeper understanding of children's thoughts and feelings about a range of challenging everyday situations. They also provide a visual tool to better support a child's emotional development and adjustment, so as to better cope with the difficulties experienced throughout life.

Developing Coping Skills in a Universal Group: Teaching Coping Skills across Various Group Settings

Coping is about going with the flow. When I am annoyed at someone, I think good thoughts, which helps me to feel good and do good. That is the motto in our classroom. *Harrison, 8 years*

Rationale

Coping skill acquisition can take place formally or informally, individually and within large or smaller group settings. This chapter will outline the importance of social and emotional competence and development for young children and considerations for teachers and practitioners when working with universal groups.

Setting the scene

Social and emotional competence is a key aspect of development and educational settings are well equipped to nurture this development. The relationship between early years emotional competence and social competence has been clearly established (Denham et al., 2003). Similarly healthy development and coping are inextricably intertwined. During the early years children need to be skilled at both managing relationships, with peers and others, and managing their emotions. Whether managing emotions or managing relationships comes first is yet to be determined. Expressiveness is a central aspect of emotional competence, along with emotional knowledge, and there are links between emotional knowledge, peer status and prosocial behaviour. Emotional regulation is a third aspect of emotional competence. The regulating of negative emotions as well as the awareness and utilization of positive emotions are both important and skilful coping is about the capacity to modify emotional reactions as the situation demands. As Denham and colleagues (2003) point out, young children often need external assistance to modify their emotional reactions. Parents and teachers have reported the links between this emotional regulatory coping and social competence (Eisenberg et al., 1995).

Denham and colleagues (2003) explored emotional competence in children aged between 3 and 4 years, following up a year later with further study. They found that emotional competence impacted social competence both at 3–4 years of age and in the subsequent year. Thus the presence of emotional competence appears to be a stable predictor of future social competence. Emotional expressiveness, particularly as it relates to happiness, works well in terms of achieving a positive reaction from both adults and other children. It is generally easier to like a happy child. Emotional knowledge at an early age predicted social competence. Not surprisingly, the strongest predictor of social competence was emotional regulation, since both emotional expressiveness and emotional knowledge are linked to emotional regulation.

Over and above emotional competence, the components of social competence include self-awareness, social awareness, responsible decision making, self-management and relationship management. Each of these can be addressed in the context of the early years' classroom.

What the adult, whether teacher or parent, says or does is important in the learning relationship. This is particularly true in group situations as the adult–child interaction is not only important for the individual but also for the group. As the adult models behaviour, social learning invariably takes place.

Carol Dweck and her associates illustrate how our attitudes about the self and our learning are formed at an early age and how school experiences play an important part. Her body of work relates to theories about children's intelligence and their mindset towards either mastery or helplessness orientation. Mastery is about belief in one's capacity to learn and to successfully complete tasks. In the socio-emotional learning environment it is more important that children develop thinking and communication skills, so they can contribute to any discussion without fear of ridicule or failure. In that way they can 'master' or learn rather than feeling foolish or helpless. This is true in the general learning environment as much as in settings where the focus is on art, music or dance.

Mindset

The impact of mindset on achievement is demonstrated by Dweck and her associates. Dweck (1998) gives clear guidelines as to the experiences that develop helplessness, as opposed to a sense of mastery with its belief that abilities are changeable. Children's sense of confidence in the learning environment comes from teachers and adults creating a climate where effort is rewarded and ideas and performances are accepted and encouraged, rather than simply praised for their quality or speed of execution. Dweck points out that it is the rewarding of effort rather than the labelling of talents or abilities that determines motivation and how goals are achieved. Perception of the self is determined by feedback after completing tasks. Rather than praise for speed and quality of execution, there needs to be acknowledgement of effort.

Think happy thoughts

Mastery-orientation

Two decades ago, in their work on learned helplessness, Hiroto and Seligman (1975), Miller and Seligman (1975), and Diener and Dweck (1978, 1980) spelled out two different reactions to failure. There are those who are helpless (give up and show deterioration in performance) and there are those who are mastery-oriented (take action to surmount problems). It is not a matter of ability but of mindset. Elliot and Dweck (1988) established that the goals students set themselves gave rise to either helplessness or mastery-oriented responses. They identified two types of goals: performance goals (which aim for favourable rather than negative judgement of competence, that is, to look smart) and learning goals (where the aim is to increase competence, that is, to get smarter) (p. 237). 'Both sets of goals are natural, necessary, and pretty much universal' (p. 238). Everyone one wants their ability to be recognized by others and everyone wants to learn new things. Elliot and Dweck repeatedly observed that performance goals, where students were focused on measuring their ability by their performance, made them vulnerable to a helpless pattern in the face of failure. In contrast, learning goals, which involved focusing on the effort and strategies needed for learning, fostered a mastery-oriented stance toward difficulty (Ames and Archer, 1988; Dweck and Leggett, 1988; Pintrich et al., 1994).

Students' theories of intelligence are associated with their goals. That is, those with performance goals see intelligence as static while those with mastery goals believe that intelligence can be developed. These two theories of intelligence have been called entity and incremental theories (Dweck and Sorich, 1999). In a series of studies they showed that different theories of intelligence set up different goals (Dweck and Leggett, 1988; Zhao et al., 1998). Entity theory fosters performance goals and helpless responses to failure, while incremental theory fosters learning goals and a mastery response. Entity theorists feel that having to work hard (show effort) risks showing that one does not have ability.

The impact of mindset on achievement was examined in Dweck's study of the transition to junior high school. Students' theories of intelligence were the best predictors of their seventh grade results. Entity theorists remained low achievers, with a pattern of helpless

Blame self

response, while incremental theorists displayed a mastery-oriented pattern. Another study (Sorich and Dweck, 1997) found that both learning and performing were important goals, but when goals were placed in conflict (as in real life), incremental theorists were far more interested in learning than simply performing well. They wanted to meet challenges and acquire new skills rather than simply perform easy work to make them look smart. Entity theorists wanted to minimize effort. They had conflicting interests. They wanted to do well, but had an aversion to the effort required. Incremental theorists believed that effort was a key ingredient to success. The mastery-oriented approach by incremental students yielded better results intellectually and emotionally.

These patterns begin as early as the preschool years, with at least one third of the students showing helpless response when experiencing failure (Cain and Dweck, 1995; Herbert and Dweck, 1985; Dweck, 1991). In kindergarten, helpless children felt 'not good' and 'not nice'. In their role-play they acted out more criticism and punishment. Furthermore, helpless young children (Heyman et al., 1992) see badness as a stable trait. It is socialization that makes a difference.

Elements to consider when working with a group

In addition to considering the important elements of social and emotional competence and the teacher's or adult's interactions with the group, teachers and group leaders will utilize a range of techniques within their repertoire with which to engage young children. These include large visual displays – using the situation or coping images placed in an enlarged format on a board or projected onto a screen; asking questions to the group or to an individual child within the group and organizing children at work stations where they collaboratively respond to questions relating to situations and coping. The interactions can be a question–answer format as outlined in the following sections or involve requesting the child to do a visual representation (see Chapter 7, Visual Arts).

Interactions: an observation of coping images in practice

Interaction 1: Teasing

Age of children: 4–5 Years
Session type: Classroom group discussion

Bullied

Teacher instruction: What do you see?
Child M: 'Somebody teasing another person.'

Child N: 'A big kid teasing a little kid because he has a toy bunny rabbit.'

Child R: 'I think the little kid had the rabbit first but the other kid snatched if off them.'

Child F: 'Maybe the big guy doesn't like pink and the little guy does and he's teasing him.'

Child P: 'I think he's teasing. I think the big kid wants it 'cause the little kid wants it.'

Teacher instruction: What do you think?
Child T: 'He must have gone into his room at night and taken it.'

Child J: 'The little kid was being naughty and the grown-up took it off him.'

⇨

Child G: 'I think the big kid was being naughty and teasing and took it off him.'

Child G: 'I think the little boy was playing at first, then the big kid took it away.'

Child A: 'I think the little kid was playing with it and the bid kid came and took it off him and said "If you don't give me that, you're not coming to my party."'

Teacher instruction: What do you feel?

Examples of children's responses: Bad, sad, angry, upset, crying, disappointment, frustrated, nervous, not good, worried.

Teacher instruction: What do you do?

Child R: 'I would say "don't do it".'

Child T: 'I would say "I don't like it and stop it now."'

Child A: 'Please stop it and walk away.'

Child J: 'I would walk away and tell the teacher.'

Child J: 'Tell my mum and dad.'

Child F: 'I would walk away and if I was at school, I would tell the teachers.'

Teachers' creative approach: Teacher held the large card up to the group and allowed children to discuss what they thought was happening, why and what they would do in this situation. Teacher reflected that she found using the smaller cards in a large group worked well. She asked the children to choose a card that interested them (a situation they have been in before) and then asked them to explain what was happening in the picture, had they ever been in this situation and how had they coped with it. It was great for children who had been in the situation but didn't offer any suggestions as to how they coped with it, as other children were able to share with that child how they had coped and suggest a range of strategies they could try. The teacher thought that it enabled the children to see that they are not alone in what they feel in different situations and that many of us deal with similar problems or anxieties and that it's okay.

Interaction 2: Making a choice

Age of children: 4 years old
Session type: Large group, circle-time
The teacher presented an image to the children of a small child having to choose between two groups of friends (this is an example of how instructors can create situation-specific images with clippings or line drawings).

Teacher instruction: What do you do?
In a whole group, discussed what was happening in the scenario. The children thought the boy didn't know whom to play with. The group discussed how he would make the choice – by the activity or the children involved.

Teacher's creative approach: The group built a discussion from the other card (friendship) and talked about how people can have more than one friend or one set of friends and that children often seem to play in different groups to have different experiences. The group gave each child in the group a name and children subsequently engaged more as a result.

What would you like to do now? (Teacher's comments): Follow-up with this card using names again to help children feel safety, empathy and familiarity. Use in outdoor area where children sometimes find it hard to choose.

Interaction 3: Friendship

Age of children: 3–4 Years
Session type: Small group situation

Wanting to belong

Teacher instruction: What do you do?
Card used for a group of seven girls who are trying to form relationships where the exchange of ideas and roles present conflict. Within the group, four girls have a bond, having been together in the centre over the previous year. Three other girls are new to the centre, with one girl knowing one of the girls from the previous year.

Session leader's creative approach (verbatim from teacher's comments): 'To bring together the girls' ideas and ways of communicating so that each of them feel part of a group and can feel able to present their ideas. The image was presented at the same time as the 'making a choice' image within a small group setting. The question initially asked of the group was, 'What is happening in each of the situations?'

1. The group indicated that the other two children were not sharing, the other child would be unhappy, sad and not have a friend.
2. Their comments were related to what was happening within their own relationships with situations when playing together.
3. To uncover how the children felt about themselves, they were asked to draw a circle on a piece of paper.
4. Next, they chose a coping image that represented their feelings about forming relationships.
5. In each of the circles, each child was asked what could they 'construct' if they were to build a three-dimensional block construction together.
6. After writing down each idea, each child was asked with whom they would join together. Each child chose a colour and drew the lines to the person they had chosen and how they would connect.
7. The diagram demonstrated that the children with dominant personalities drew bigger circles than the quieter, more reserved children. Also, certain children joined only with a restricted selection of other children.
8. The group then joined each of their ideas together in a circle, leaving no parts isolated.

Other ways in

'Ways in' may be introduced in various settings or activities that occur normally within a child's experience at school. Consider introducing the cards during:

- circle time
- a restorative justice session
- a reflection exercise
- a group role-play
- free time (or break times)

Additional questions that may prompt discussions could include the following:

- What would you do, feel, think?
- What have you done in the past?
- What would you like to do differently?
- What would others do, feel, think?

Final thoughts

Coping interventions, whether incidental, in the family context, in the classroom, or through structured sessions, assist the development of young people's critical thinking skills and an awareness of themselves and others. Notwithstanding this, children are also being helped to acquire skills of language and mastery of everyday problems and situations. An environment that stimulates deep thinking and general acceptance of thoughts and ideas leads to the best outcomes.

Learning activities can take place in a large group setting or within a smaller grouping of young people where the focus is on addressing a particular problem. Settings will vary greatly with regard to what is possible and most appropriate. The following section, Part II: Moving, Thinking Doing: Applications and Activities across Disciplines and Settings outlines applied activities across various disciplines that can be adapted to most group settings, whether large or small.

PART 2
Moving, Thinking, Doing: Applications and Activities across Disciplines and Settings

Visual Arts: Developing Coping Skills through Art and Play

Red is angry, blue is water and green is relax. *Dillon, 4 years*

Rationale

Young children's drawings and paintings provide deep insight into their thinking and imaginings. This chapter will provide guidance for teachers and clinicians as to how they can help young children to make their thinking visible through two- and three-dimensional art practices. Ideas, feelings and strong emotions can be expressed using a range of media that help to make personal marks and statements that express understandings.

Setting the scene

Taking an arts perspective: perceiving, thinking and processing

The arts provide us with a unique way of 'knowing' or experiencing the world. In all cultures, the arts offer important ways of expressing and representing ideas, emotions, values and spiritual beliefs and as such are legitimately grouped as a key area of human learning and activity. Within educational settings the arts are recognized as 'symbol systems' or modes of communication that are used in organized ways through cultural practice to express and communicate meanings. From this perspective a number of eminent scholars (Cassirer, 1953; Gardner, 1994; Eisner, 2002) have investigated symbol systems as a distinctive feature of human cognition, offering an insight into the link between the biological, namely 'the nervous system with its structures and functions' and the cultural with its 'roles and activities' (Gardner, 1983 p. 301). Thus, for the young child, symbolization or artistic expression is a form of knowing about the world; the child draws on information coming from the senses as well as thoughts, feelings and imagination.

Any investigation of the arts requires an understanding of thinking, namely how does the mind create? Eisner (2002, p. 2) acknowledges that humans are 'sentient creatures born into a qualitative environment in and through which they live' and hence he places great emphasis on the relationship between sensory or perceptual experience and thinking, citing the senses as the 'first avenues to consciousness'. He sees cognition as a generic process of coming to know the world through the senses and he identifies the arts as playing an important role in refining the sensory system and cultivating imaginative capabilities. The learning process for the child is dependent on sensory input and involves perceptual activity followed by the abstraction of a wide range of sensory concepts that are made available from the environment. It is through the abstraction of each of the sensory modalities that concepts are formed. This process depends upon a 'constructive' use of cognition whereby concepts are formed and then joined with other concepts. Thus the child makes sense of the environment, predicts probability patterns and regulates interactions with it. Eisner believes that it is this process of construction and abstraction that is at the root of art and forms the basis of thinking and knowing. He points out, however, that 'the sensory system does not work alone; it requires for its development the tools of culture: language, the arts, science, values and the like. With the aid of culture we learn to create ourselves' (2002, p. 2).

It is clear that the arts provide concrete models of human experience; a type of knowledge that is simply not accessible in other forms;

a combination of logical processing and other less tangible elements of thinking such as imagination, empathy, creativity spontaneity and commitment. Therefore, the young child while learning through the arts is accessing a form of non-verbal thought in action (Dewey, 1934) with self-expression and individuality being central elements of the art-making.

Exemplars

Representing thinking through visual representation: acknowledging the voice of the child

Through the UN Convention on the Rights of the Child (UNCRC, 1989) a new view of children has emerged, one that acknowledges children's participation in all matters affecting their lives. Children today are viewed as active citizens who are capable of independent articulation of ideas and interests and as such there is an understanding that they should not only have the right to be heard but should be given as many opportunities as possible for participation in all areas of their life. Article 12 of the Convention, states:

> State parties shall assure to the child who is capable of forming his or her own views freely in all matters affecting the child, the views of the child being given due weight in accordance with the age and maturity of the child. (UNCRC, 1989)

Article 13 draws further attention to the need for young children to be provided with opportunities for self-expression in as many ways as possible. It states:

> The child shall have the right to freedom of expression; this right shall include freedom to seek, receive and impart information and ideas of all kinds, regardless of frontiers, either orally, in writing or in print, in the form of art, or through any other media of the child's choice. (UNCRC, 1989)

In support of these principles there is a growing body of literature (Cremin and Slatter, 2004; Dockett and Perry, 2005; Leonard, 2006) that identifies the importance of providing opportunities for the voice of the young child to be heard. Contemporary teaching methodologies including the Mosaic Approach[1] (Clark and Moss, 2001) 'draw and tell conversations' (Driessnack, 2006) and 'drawing–telling' (Wright, 2003) have been developed to support the documentation of children's thoughts, feelings and ideas.

Linking language and art-making

Research indicates that verbal language plays a vital role in learning, with Vygotsky (1962) identifying 'verbal thought' as the intersection between thinking and speech. Dewey's (1934) seminal ideas on the nature of learning have been influential for many decades. Dewey acknowledged art-making as a direct form of experience; a form of non-verbal thought in action where an integration of the intellectual, physical, emotional and sensory modalities occurs. There can be no doubt that communication through visual art offers individuals a non-verbal symbolic language through which to tell stories and to tap into their private and personal worlds of real and imagined thoughts and ideas. Holliday and colleagues (2009) cite several authors who comment on the power of drawing as a tool for young children to externalize their thoughts or make their ideas visible.

Creating images is the outward display of thinking. It provides an accessible multimodal method of learning coping skills and over the years children's drawings have been used extensively in the fields of education, psychology and psychiatry as a way of gaining insight into their thinking and emotional states. Rollins (2005) argues that a child's drawing can be a window not only into the child's feelings but also into cognitive and developmental maturity, coping styles and personality. Other authors (Dockett and Perry, 2005; Clark and Moss, 2001) highlight the importance of listening to children's comments as they draw, in order to capture a true picture of how they may be thinking or feeling about matters that concern them. Such an approach places emphasis on the cognitive or emotional message being conveyed rather than on the fine motor skill or aesthetic representation skills and outcomes of the child's marks. When children are given the opportunity to create their image

---

1. The Mosaic approach is a multi-method approach in which children's drawings and the like can be used in conjunction with talk and observation to gain deeper understanding of children's perspectives.

and add their verbal comment, they in essence own their representation and interpretation beyond the influence of either parent or teacher.

Drawing is a natural mode of expression for young children and provides an immediate starting point for conversation. Coates (2002) has uncovered that drawing and talking go hand in hand and that young children often engage in self-talk as they draw, creating free-flow narratives that express their immediate thoughts about the idea or feeling being explored. Jung (1964) argued that communication through art provides an opportunity for the expression of the psychological state of the individual with creative representations bringing relief and providing for the concretization of internally experienced emotionally charged feelings and thoughts.

Using drawing to support coping skills

The emotional health of individuals is essentially informed by the balance that is achieved through internal processes and how they are impacted by the context within which the individual operates. Young children growing and developing in a social environment are, according to Vygotsky (1986), constantly problem solving and compelled by the very nature of this activity to formulate their ideas verbally, a process that enables them to begin the act of self-directed monitoring. Creating space for direct experience in art-making in a supportive and empathetic relationship allows the young child to feel comfortable and safe to explore significant personal issues or concerns. The experience begins with the child being provided with art materials that provide the tool for experiential art-making that helps to develop self-awareness through the isolation and development of prominent ideas and interests. The experience is further extended when overlaid with language; parents and teachers can initiate and help extend conversations that help make feelings and experiences concrete. The task then involves the easily accessible combination of drawing and/or writing and talking (Betensky, 1995; Lett, 1995); a combination that encourages personalized verbal sharing, imagery and written words. These work together to create a meaningful relationship between what is perceived and what is expressed, with the description of the drawing providing an opening for learning and understandings to develop from the experience being recorded.

Encouraging the development of coping skills using reflective drawing/telling

One of the paramount aims of working with young children around social and emotional issues is to help them develop the ability to relate to 'the self' and they do this through being involved in activities that encourage self-reflection. Being helped by adults to understand the relationship that exists between the inner self and the outer world is the first step to developing the coping skills important for personal development and growth in all relationships. As mentioned earlier, Vygotsky (1962) has determined that words and thoughts are inseparable, with words being considered a tool that enables individuals to manage and share their perceptual experiences. Hence for young children, being encouraged to draw and then describe what is seen in the artwork is one way of tapping into inner realties and, as Wright (2003, p. 24) points out:

> Communicating via drawing and storytelling gives children the opportunity to create and share meaning using two modes – the non-verbal (i.e. graphic depiction stemming from imagery and visual memory) in collaboration with the verbal (i.e. creating a story that accompanies their artwork).

The process, which takes place within a trusting and empathetic environment, aims to cater for increased awareness and understanding of a number of human dimensions, namely:

- beliefs, or in other words the ideas, values, attitudes and opinions that an individual child might hold;
- feelings and sensations which include emotional responses such as fears, anger, anxieties;
- actions and interactions which are the intentional or purposeful behaviours within the social context to influence how an individual feels about him or herself and how individual actions impact on others; and
- creative imagery capabilities that draw on the imagination and stored memories of past or present experiences and even projections into the future.

For parents and teachers, 'drawing/telling' is a strategy that supports the development of 'habits of mind' or 'thinking habits' that are integrated and holistic. Eisner (2002, p. 3) believes that any exploration through the arts provides opportunities for 'expanding our consciousness, shaping our dispositions, satisfying our quest for thinking, establishing contact with others, and sharing our culture'. The combination of visual art and verbal response provides for a range of skill development. In the first instance children are developing the craft of drawing and/or writing. They are encouraged to focus, engage and persist with the problem that is posed and they are also encouraged to envision the problem and imagine solutions. The activity supports the development of reflective thinking skills where questioning and explanation help children to learn to think and talk with others about their feelings. Such activity stretches the imagination and helps children to identify their capacities and to potentially learn from their mistakes or accidents.

Drawing/telling and the coping images

Research across a variety of fields (Diem-Wille, 2001; Piscitelli and Anderson, 2001) has highlighted the power of children's drawings for their capacity to provide insight into children's constructions of their educational, social, cultural and emotional worlds. When combined with personalized interpretative verbal responses children are provided with a multimodal opportunity to express thoughts, ideas and feelings. Such an approach caters for those children who are more suited to the communication of their meanings and understandings using symbolic representation and it is relatively straightforward for parents or teachers to use the technique with children either individually or in groups. The procedures include discussion followed by reflective drawing, which can be accompanied by interpretative verbal/written analysis.

Discussion of the situation and coping images

Introduce the situation or coping card to the child or children by laying the images out on the floor. Ask the child or children to take a close look at the pictures and choose one that can form the basis of discussion. Leading, open-ended questions are used to guide the opening discussion:

- What do you see happening in this picture?
- Why do you think that this is happening?
- What do you think the child is feeling?

- Why do you think the child is feeling this way?
- Do you think this child has spoken to anyone about his /her problem?
- Can you think of what might help the child to feel better?
- Has this situation ever happened to you?
- How did you feel?
- How did you make yourself feel better?
- Did you ask a friend to help you?
- Did you ask an adult?

Usually 15 minutes is an adequate amount of time for the children to respond to the questions and maintain their focus on the discussion

Reflective drawing/telling and interpretation

The above guidelines provide the impetus for the drawing task that takes place immediately following the discussion. An A4 paper and black fine liner, lead pencils and coloured crayons are provided and children are asked to draw a picture of the situation that has been discussed. Upon completion they are asked to provide an explanation of their drawing, which is written by the child either on the back of the drawing or on a separate piece of paper. Such an approach allows for the parent or teacher to enter more fully into the reality of the child's world, with the children's verbal interpretative explanations providing even deeper access into their perceptions, thoughts and lived experience.

If children find it difficult to provide an explanation of the drawing, parents or teachers can help by asking:

- Who is in this drawing?
- What is this part of the drawing telling me?
- Why did you choose to draw about this?
- Has this happened to you?
- How did you feel?

Analysing the reflective drawing/telling

The above approach can be used regularly to collect information about how individual children are representing their understandings of their world and their experiences. Each child has a unique story to tell and each drawing and verbal interchange provides information about personal, social, emotional and cultural histories. As Kendrick and McKay

(2009, pp. 57–8) argue, adults can 'view these drawings as 'pivotal' lessons learned in our ability to understand more fully what the children are able to communicate about the diverse ways they see themselves and others'.

Drawing/tellings can be taken on face value for what they say and the following case study provides insight into how young children talk through their responses to a stressful situation.

It was the beginning of the school year and a small group of 4-year-old children were introduced to the 'saying goodbye' image.

The teacher began the introductory discussion by asking the children: What can you see happening in this picture?

> **Abby:** The mum is happy and the boy is sad.
>
> **Xuan:** I think that the boy is waving to his mumma and the mumma is waving back. She's happy because the boy is going to school.

Saying goodbye

James: He doesn't want to go to school. He's feeling sad because he doesn't want to go.

Ginger: I think that he wants to go back home. Maybe his mum is going to work.

The teacher then expanded the discussion by asking: Have you ever felt this way?

Abby: I sometimes feel sad having to say goodbye to my mummy when I go to kinder. I have to try and feel better. My mum reads me a book.

Xuan: If I don't say goodbye to mum and I don't give dada a kiss and cuddle I miss him.

James: I felt sad last time because my mum was going. I wanted to give her a cuddle but she was gone.

The teacher then asked the children to draw about a time when they had to say goodbye to their mother or father. They were provided with A4 paper and black fine liner pens.

Drawing/telling Ordine

I'm saying goodbye to my mum and my mum's going to work. I want her to stay with me and then I feel sad, but when she is here I feel happy. I feel happy when I take a deep breath.

Drawing/telling Ginger

It's my mum saying goodbye and I'm happy because she gave me a cuddle and she always gives me a cuddle.

Drawing/telling Anika

That's me and my mum and my mum doesn't want to say goodbye to me, so I'm feeling sad. Then she goes to work and then I still feel sad because she is not here. I don't feel sad all day once I cheer up.

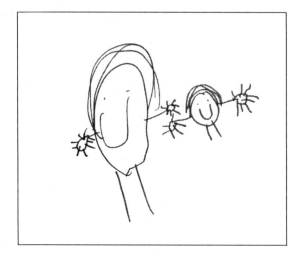

Drawing/telling Harriet

Well my mum is feeling sad because she has to leave me at kinder, but I am feeling happy.

Drawing/telling Max

This is me and the big one is mum.

Mum was about to open the door when suddenly she turned around and when she turned around she saw me working somewhere and I was happy.

Well, my mum is feeling sad because she has to leave me at kinder, but I'm feeling happy.

A cautionary note:

Teachers and parents are not encouraged to probe or to interpret. Clinicians who are trained in interpreting children's drawings may encourage more reflection and may utilize the children's drawings for extended discussion.

Taking this approach in a social setting encourages the shared cognition that Vygotsky (1962) talks about in his Zone of Proximal Development theory whereby new or developed understandings are created through collaborative inquiry. Children usually listen very intently to the ideas of their peers, at times taking on the ideas of others and making them their own. Quite often children draw their own rendition of an idea being expressed by a friend and in this scenario one clearly sees how the child's interpersonal learning is enriched and deepened through dialogic (visual and verbal) inter-change. Once the young child is able to give symbolic form to an idea a new world opens. It is a world where focused concentration on an easily accessible task allows for meta-cognitive thinking which includes the recording of perceptual experience, recalling memo-ries, thinking and planning for the future and making creative con-nections between parts. Hence, drawing/telling allows children to organize their thoughts in a concrete way and to develop ideas to a more complex level. It is clear that the interplay between interper-sonal and intrapersonal dialogue plays an important role in helping to support higher order thinking skills.

Other ways in

Another approach that helps the young child connect with their emotions draws on the understanding of how emotions are expressed through the face.

Using the coping images the teacher focused the children's atten-tion on the facial expressions of the characters in the images.

T: Take a close look at the child's face. How do you think he is feeling?

As an extension to the activity the children were then introduced to Picasso's painting titled the 'Weeping Woman' and asked:

T: How do you think that the person in the painting is feeling?

T: Take a mirror and look at your own face. See if you can change your face to feel sad, happy, angry?

T: Look at how the shape of your eyes, mouth, your eyebrows change when you change your face from a happy face to an angry face.

T: How do you think that you can use lines, colour and shape to draw a sad, happy or angry face?

Final thoughts

From these examples it is clear that the combination of coping images and drawing/telling provides children with an opportunity to express their upsets both verbally and through their symbolic representations. The statements that children make when guided by an empathetic adult provide a true reflection of their personal thoughts, ideas and feelings. By 'listening' to the voices of young children as expressed through their art and words parents and teachers are given a privileged insight into the young child's emotional world.

6 Dance: Learning Coping Skills through Music and Movement

When I am angry I shout like this . . . dah-gah-rah! Really loud. I feel better when I dance. I feel happy when Mum stops growling. *Milo, 4 years*

Rationale

The body is one of the young child's tools for learning about the world. Explorations through movement provide opportunities for developing understanding about the self, others and the environment. In this light, dance provides an enjoyable and readily accessible medium for the expression of ideas, thoughts and feelings.

Setting the scene

As Hanna (1979) states 'to dance is human' and in many ways expressive movement can be viewed as a universal language of children who use it to discover and learn about their world, make meaning of experience and to express reactions and ideas to others and situations. As such it is a unifying activity that allows individuals to develop self-awareness and to learn to be sensitive to the needs and feelings of others. Young children love to dance – to move rhythmically and to move more precisely and more fully than in everyday life. Dance enlivens the senses, stimulating vitality and energy for creative and expressive problem solving. It is also a very effective tool for expressing emotion and consequently an appropriate teaching method that enables teachers to help support children's explorations of a range of situations that may cause stress or anxiety. Research indicates that the physical, emotional and psychological benefits of learning through dance in a social context are many, and it is clear that expressive movement provides young children with an opportunity to interpret their ideas, feelings and sensory impressions through their bodies. Being able to transform internal and external images, thoughts and sensations into a concrete form through dance is one way young children can problem solve and formulate their ideas physically, visually and verbally, within a social situation.

Modern Educational Dance was first published in the United Kingdom by the 'father of modern dance theory', Rudolf Laban (1879–1958) who was particularly interested in the relationship between the body, movement and the human mind, expounding the idea of 'movement consciousness' which resulted in dance being understood from the viewpoint of its affective contribution to the development of the moving/feeling/being individual (Smith-Autard, 2004). Laban's influence has been extensive, with many prominent early dance educators (Russel 1975; Boorman, 1969, 1973; Exiner and Lloyd, 1973, 1981; Stinson, 1988) being influenced by and adopting his ideas for the teaching of dance. These trailblazing educators believed passionately in the value of dance as an art form that provided children with the opportunity to express their inner selves and as an important area of study that should be taught to all children. Outcomes attributed to dance were identified and these included critical thinking, social skill development and increased understanding and sensitivity to feeling states. Most importantly these dance educators identified the value of dance as a vehicle for personal expression that could be made available to all and not just a talented few. The underlying belief was that every person is unique having the ability for expressive communication and for those teachers working within the discipline the 'fixing and retaining of movement patterns had no special value' (Exiner and Lloyd, 1973, p. 3) but rather the everyday movement vocabulary of the individual became the material for dance improvisation. As Pugh McCutchen (2006, p. 5) states 'educational dance is for all children: it broadly educates, it embraces all aspects of dance that have educational value, it increases aesthetic education and it affects the total education of the child. Educational dance is dance that educates and inspires the young. It stretches the body and the mind'. Broadly speaking, creative educational dance can be defined as the interpretation and expression of a child's ideas, feelings and sensory impressions expressed symbolically through natural, spontaneous and individual movement forms.

Drawing on wide ranging influences, creative educational dance has at its core 'dance as art', with the major concern being the production of formed and performed objects for aesthetic enjoyment. It brings into focus a framework that includes creating, performing and appreciating that provides opportunities for creative, imaginative and personalized experiential learning where the emphasis is placed on process; and learning that combines the affective alongside the development of new knowledge, skills and techniques.

This theory of creating, performing and appreciating is the approach used to achieve the art of dance in education. It offers opportunities for children to explore and communicate ideas, thoughts and feelings and at the same time facilitates creative thinking including imagining, improvising, problem solving, developing a movement vocabulary, decision making, selecting, sequencing, refining and appreciating (Wright, 2003; Smith-Autard, 2004). In relation to children viewing the dance of others, such an experience allows for the development of more sophisticated sensory awareness and encourages meta-cognition through an analytical process that involves the use of descriptive language, interpretation and critical judgements that fosters reflection upon personal creations and those of others.

Psychological–social learning in dance

It is during the early years that children begin to understand who they are in relation to others. It is at this time that they move away from their parents expanding social relationships and taking on the developmental task of building friendships with peers. Interactions between children of this age are seen to promote a range of cognitive and learning skills with competence in cooperative play, taking turns, sharing and understanding the perspective of others gradually developing over time. A recent study undertaken by Lobo and Winsler (2006) has provided strong empirical evidence for the effectiveness of dance in supporting the development of both self-confidence and social competence, with the study highlighting the reduction in behaviour problems of participating children over the course of the eight-week programme.

As identified by Chappell and Young (2007) the link between individual learning dispositions and self-concept is also relevant. The psychological life of all individuals is impacted both by the intra-subjective and the inter-subjective experience and for young children learning through dance provides an opportunity for internal images, thoughts and sensations to be transformed into a concrete form. Experiential involvement in dance facilitates processing of the internal psychological experience of each participant with problem solving in a social situation compelling the children to formulate their ideas both physically, visually and verbally; a process that enables them to begin the act of self-directed learning. Vygotsky (1962, p. 86) refers to this as the 'zone of proximal development', which he defines as:

> The distance between the actual development level as determined by independent problem solving and the level of potential development as determined through problem solving under adult guidance or in collaboration with more capable peers.

Through participation in dance the intra-subjective and inter-subjective relationship between the children and the teachers is established through several processes including direct sensory rich movement experience, the teaching of skills and techniques to develop the children's movement and choreographic repertoire and opportunities through observation and drawing/telling (Betensky, 1995; Lett, 1995), with a supportive empathetic teacher who empowers individuals to reflect on the experience.

Alongside the psychological–social domain of learning in dance sits aesthetic perception, which is defined by Pugh McCutchen (2006, p. 257) as 'seeing with the eyes of the heart'. Dewey (1934) reminds us that 'all thinking and thoughtful action, as experienced moment-to-moment, are emotionally qualified' and this idea is exemplified in children's learning in dance where dance as art can inspire because it speaks to the body–mind–sprit of the doer and viewer. Theorists (Lavender and Predcock-Linnell, 2001; Redfern, 1983) agree that engaging the aesthetic self calls on the highest order of critical thinking that bringing together perceptual information from the senses, physical refinement in motion in the form of kinaesthetic understandings and the complete use of psychological skills while incorporating ways of knowing. It is at this point that it is clear that learning in dance is a holistic and integrated experience where aesthetic experience has the ability to elevate the ordinary to the extraordinary; the challenge is for the teachers of dance to help children to see the sensory qualities inherent in movement and to avoid not drawing attention to the hidden meanings for which there is no language.

A bounty of benefits

Research indicates that the physical, emotional and psychological benefits of learning through dance in a social context are many, and it is clear that expressive movement provides young children with an opportunity to interpret their ideas, feelings and sensory impressions through their bodies. Being able to transform internal and external images, thoughts and sensations into a concrete form through dance is one way young children can problem solve and formulate their ideas physically, visually and verbally, within a social situation.

Delving into dance

Working with dance is straightforward; all that is required is a willingness on behalf of the educational professional, whether they are a teacher or clinician, to turn everyday human movement into something special by 'linking movements rhythmically, spatially, bodily, dynamically and artfully so they connect and flow together in order for the movement to transform into dance' (McCutchen, 2006, p. 129). The practitioner must also be prepared to be fully involved with the movement and the children, guiding and responding as the movement stories are established and responses generated.

Exemplars

A session plan

The dance class

In any dance class teachers can simply think about the movement content as being:

- What you do or the movement activities you choose: everyday actions such as breathing, walking, running, rolling, standing, stretching, collapsing, and the like using a range of body parts and body shapes?
- How you move or the dynamic quality of your movements: moving quickly, slowly, strongly, lightly, heavily?
- Where is the space around you – in place, or through the space, up, down, sideways, forwards, backwards?
- Who or what you move with – dancing alone, with a partner or group or an object?

It is useful to have a standard session framework that accommodates varied dance content associated with the chosen situation or coping image. The following structure can be used as a guide:

Welcome the children into an uncluttered space and gather them together on an attractive piece of material where you can say hello, share news, introduce the situation or coping image content of the class, create a visual mind map of the ideas or issues associated with the selected image or encourage preliminary discussion about the issue to be explored. This is the time to gather and organize thoughts, identify which task is going to be undertaken, brainstorm ideas around the topic and make a decision as to which ideas the group is going to follow. This space becomes the 'safe place' where children can regularly return during the class and sit to enjoy the dances of others.

Let's do it! Introduce the warm-up by inviting the children into the space to make a 'starting body shape'. During this part of the class encourage the children to 'sense' their bodies in movement and stillness, in parts and as a whole and also to watch and listen to any musical stimuli that you might use.

Initiate whole group movement exploration by introducing the movement content selected during the Scared of the dark exercise on page 86. Using a guided improvisation approach, support children's explorations of the movement qualities. Expand the experience through questioning, verbal and physical suggestions, teacher modelling and social contagion.

Sequence the movement material by modelling a series of movements that work together to tell the story. Provide appropriate musical accompaniment, either with percussion instruments or taped music.

Organize small group improvisations by dividing the children into groups and giving them an opportunity to perform their personal responses for each other. Half the group dances and the other half return to the 'safe haven' as audience. Use the thinking strategy: 'what do you see, what do you feel about that and what do you wonder about it' as a way of guiding the children's feedback and evaluation of the experience.

To conclude the session invite the children to enjoy solo 'free dance'. This is a time for the children to 'dance any way they like' with the practitioner providing appropriate musical accompaniment. The *humdrum* offers great accompaniment for this.

Finally, the children can enjoy a short period of relaxation during which they can find a space in the room to lie. The main purpose of this part of the class is to allow children a chance to unwind. Quiet, relaxing music helps establish a relaxing and reflective ambience.

Reflective drawing

The practitioner can offer reflective drawing/telling by distributing drawing boards and A4 white paper and black fine liner pens. The children can be asked 'to draw something remembered from the class today'. Upon completion of the drawings the practitioner either asks the children to write their own sentence on their drawing or moves about the room writing the child-generated stories on each drawing.

The practitioner can ask each child to comment on what he or she has learned during the class.

Corresponding body movements to coping images

Experiential involvement in dance facilitates processing of the internal psychological experience of each participant. Problem solving in a social situation compels children to formulate their ideas physically, visually and verbally; enabling them to begin the process of self-directed learning that communicates ideas, thoughts and feelings. It is clear that finding an expressive voice through dance provides children with an accessible way of managing their personal feelings. They often need to express what is going on in their lives using dance as a cathartic activity – many powerful dances can be created from deeply felt emotion!

Dance is the art of body movement and because it involves physical action it can often lead into dramatic exploration where the unearthing of difficult issues or challenging situations can be the stimulus for the exploration of a range of symbols or metaphors. As such, dance accommodates individual and varied interpretations that in turn lead to the non-verbal problem solving. The aim is for the dance session to provide a completely safe, non-judgemental space, which helps children through a process of self-development. Research indicates that self-esteem tends to increase greatly when non-verbal modes of communication are explored. Using situation and coping images the practitioner can help children explore their emotions using everyday movement activities that allow for expressive communication in response to the dramatic scenarios depicted in the images.

The practitioner selects a situation image that is appropriate for the individual or group of children, matches the emotional content of the depicted scenario with movement content and then shapes the lesson as described earlier. The following provides guidance on how to match the situations with everyday movement activities.

Situation images

Saying goodbye – walking, waving, struggling, hugging, rocking
Scared of the dark – shivering, shaking, quivering
Sibling not playing fair – twisting, jumping, travelling on, struggling
Choosing a group/joining in – walking, looking, creeping, sliding

Being in trouble

Being reprimanded by a teacher – shrugging, spinning, freezing, retreating, melting

Change – rising, sinking, floating

Coping images

Helping others/playing – stepping, turning, lifting, bouncing, circling

Blame others – stamping, leaping, sneaking, hitting

Self-blame – curling up, hiding, crouching

Think happy thoughts –skipping, swinging, sliding, leaping

Hug a toy – swaying, bouncing, skipping, embracing

Keep feelings to self – freezing, pressing, sinking, rolling

Complain of pain – pressing, rolling, flinching

Play –whirling, falling, leaping, swaying, turning

Talk to an adult – opening, closing, standing, kneeling, walking, turning

Work hard – circling, running, moving, stopping

Worry – twisting, wringing, writhing, curling up

Hide – shaking, creeping, being still

Run away – running, hiding, jumping over

Scream – stamping, arching, shaking

Blame/self-worry

Using questioning and problem solving

Questioning is a strategy that practitioners can use to set the scene prior to beginning the active part of the session. Questioning is designed to

- find out what children already know
- stimulate curiosity and discovery
- motivate and stimulate thinking and problem solving
- focus children's attention on the content of the lesson and its essential aspects
- encourage personal reflection
- support the development of self-confidence and make children feel safe and comfortable
- evaluate the children's understandings
- inform future planning.

During the welcome section of the lesson the instructor can introduce the selected card and introduce a number of prepared and focused questions that will shape the direction of the class such as:

- What can you see in this picture?
- What do you think this child is feeling?
- What do you think the adult in the picture is saying to the child?

- What is the child saying to the adult?
- What can we do to help make this child feel better?

By asking such questions the instructor is helping the children to gather and organize their thinking about the scenario represented in the chosen image and to begin the process of problem solving. Questioning can become more in-depth and linked to the development of a mind map that will also include movement material, for example:

- How do we move when we are feeling scared of the dark?
- Can we think of movements that would help us to create a dance about this picture?
- What instruments or vocal sounds can we use to accompany our dance?

Remember that questions can be about the following:

- The situation image.
- The coping strategies images.
- The movement activities.
- How the body feels or moves?
- The quality of the movement to express the emotion depicted on the card.
- How the body moves in the space?
- Connections with others.

Lesson schema: Scared of the dark

Introduction
- Let's look at the 'Scared of the dark' image:
- What do you see in the picture?
- What is the boy feeling?
- Have you ever felt like this?
- Let's write down all the feelings that we have had (mind map).
- What makes you feel scared at night?

Warm-up
- Show me a scared face.
- What do your eyes, eyebrows, jaw, forehead feel like and look like?

Fear of the dark

- Change your face and show me another scared face.
- Stand slowly and make your whole body look scared.
- How does your body feel?
- When you hear your name, move into the space and make a scared shape.
- On the sound of the drum make another scared shape.
- Change your position and with two big steps show me another scared shape.

Exploration of movement material

- Let's warm up our scared bodies.
- Let's try shivering . . . shiver, shiver, shiver, freeze.
- Shiver to the sound of the cymbal.
- Remember we said our bodies shake when we are scared.
- Let's try shaking.
- Shake to the sound of the tambourine.
- We also said our bodies quiver when we are scared.
- Let's try quivering.
- Is this different to shivering?

Small group improvisation
- Let's join with a friend and try quivering, shaking and shivering together.
- Let's make a small group and try quivering, shaking and shivering together.
- Freeze your movements when you hear the loud sound.
- Try making a scared dance that begins slowly and gathers speed and strength to reach a climax in a frozen shape.
- Are you really feeling scared?
- Let's try some being 'Scared of the dark' dances using our quivering, shivering, shaking movements.

Whole group dance

- Let's all pretend to hide under this material.
- It's just like hiding under the blanket when you feel scared (practitioner to use a large piece of light transparent cloth).
- I'll play the cymbal and you can all group together under the material shivering, quivering and shaking together. When the cymbal stops you stop.

Individual dances

Now I'd like half the class to sit back in the 'safe place' and we'll watch the dances of the other half of the class performing their 'Scared of the dark' dances.

Reflection

- What did you see?
- How were the dancers moving?
- How did their dances make you feel?
- Repeat individual dances and reflection by changing over the groups.

Free dance

- Now it's time for everyone to move into the space.
- We need to find a solution to our scared feelings.
- What sort of dance will we make?
- I'll play the humdrum and you dance a happy carefree dance.

- What do you need to do to make yourself feel happy and carefree?
- What sort of movements will you choose?

Relaxation

- Everyone find a place to lie down on the floor, close your eyes and relax your bodies.
- Practitioner to choose relaxing music and undertake guided relaxation.

Drawing/telling

While children are resting, the teacher distributes A4 paper on a clipboard and a pencil to each child. Children are invited to draw something they have remembered from the dance class.

- What coping image did we explore?
- What movements do you remember?
- What feelings did you experience?
- How do you feel now?

Draw a picture of what happened for you in the class and I will come around to all of you to help you write your story about being scared in the dark.

Other ways in

In any dance session educational professionals, teachers or clinicians can simply think about the movement content as being:

- What you do or the movement activities you choose: everyday actions such as breathing, walking, running, rolling, standing, stretching, collapsing, and so on using a range of body parts and body shapes?
- How you move or the dynamic quality of your movements: moving quickly, slowly, strongly, lightly, heavily?
- Where is the space around you – in place, or through the space, up, down, sideways, forwards, backwards?
- Who or what you move with – dancing alone, with a partner or group or an object?

Final thoughts

Learning through dance in a social situation provides a unique tool for creative self-expression and promotes a wide range of outcomes as follows:

- opportunities for the bodily communication of feelings and thoughts
- relationship building
- co-sharing of problems with important others through bodily kinaesthetic exploration
- opportunities for the uncovering of otherwise hidden issues
- critical thinking and problem solving
- aesthetic decision making.

Dance brings together and energizes the connection between body, mind and spirit, providing a creative outlet for the emotions and for the self.

Music: Feeling, Creating and Coping with Sounds and Rhythms

When my brother picks on me a lot I feel so angry I could punch him in the face. To feel better and calm down, I go away and play on my ipod. Music helps a lot. *Alex, 11 years*

Rationale

Musical behaviours are evident very early in life with research indicating strong connections between music and behavioural responses. Linking coping to music can provide teachers and clinicians with a pleasurable and easily accessible avenue for exploring a continuum of emotional states.

Setting the scene

Music is a universal human activity which involves the organization of sound to communicate intellectual, social and emotional meanings. It is considered to be an important language of childhood (Edwards et al., 1998; Barrett, 2005; Hedges, 2004) as well as an expression of personal and social culture. In light of Eisner's (2002) idea that humans are sentient beings who are biologically designed to be sensitive to a wide range of stimuli within the environment, young children are understandably spontaneously attracted to both environmental sounds and music. Exploration of these concepts leads to a more sophisticated categorization of qualities and a deeper understanding of how the expressive communication of ideas and thoughts can find reality and form. Engaging with music, therefore, offers individuals opportunities for participation in a readily accessible communication mode; one that supports the development of 'a way of knowing' that influences how they respond to and interpret the world and express views about their experience of it.

It is widely acknowledged that young children respond to music with great enthusiasm, making it a learning modality that should be nurtured as part of everyday experience. Research indicates that babies in utero actually attend to music and learn while listening to it. Malloch (1999, 2000) talks about mother–infant communication as a form of emotional musicality, with such activities as rocking and humming (Trevarthen, 2002) offering comfort and security and playing a significant role in the attachment process. Parental singing is also cited as having a profound impact on early attachment. Trehub (2001) and Wright (2003) both propose that young children are biologically predisposed to respond to and interpret musical stimuli.

Learning through music caters for all areas of a child's development. This includes the physical, social, emotional and intellectual, with a range of long-term benefits such as the development of listening skills, higher forms of reasoning and improved spatial intelligence (Sloboda and Deliege, 1996).

The acquisition of musical understanding has also been linked to the development of other literacies, particularly language; the argument being that it employs similar cognitive processes and developments. Vygotsky (1962) argues that language is central to the development of thought and that a range of expressive communication forms help ideas, thoughts and feelings find reality and form. Eisner (2002) also points out that 'as individuals become increasingly imaginative and technically competent at transforming concepts and their associated meanings into forms, the use and the growth of the mind are revealed' (p. 22). He argues strongly for experience through the arts, highlighting the importance of children developing understandings through the manipulation of a range of symbolic codes of communication that support 'meaning making'.

A number of authors also point to a close connection between the musical development of young children and its impact on other areas of development such as language and literacy (Anvari et al., 2002), verbal memory (Ho et al., 2003), kinaesthetic, spatial, mathematics and importantly the individual's ability to relate to and empathize with others. Studies have shown that listening to music influences the listener's current subjective emotional state. If opportunities are provided for involvement in music, emotions and moods can be modulated, attention and concentration can be improved and social relationships can be generated and maintained (von Georgi et al., 2006). This extensive research demonstrates that broadly based engagement with music provides opportunities for explorations of not only sound, its qualities and how it is made, but music as an expression of personal thoughts, ideas and emotions. As teachers grapple with the demands of ensuring positive holistic development for diverse groups of children, it is clear that effective learning cannot occur without social and emotional skill competency. It is worth noting that the same set of skills that support emotional confidence and security, as well as social confidence and success, also predict school readiness and academic achievement as children grow and mature (Skewes and Thompson, 1998). With this understanding teachers are prioritizing opportunities for young children to develop a strong sense of self, responsibility for themselves and others and prosocial behaviours using music. Making sounds, singing, exploring musical games and listening to music all play a part in helping to achieve these outcomes.

A sense of self: how music can support development?

A positive sense of self in a young child manifests itself by a display of personal confidence across a wide range of social situations and through independent action with everyday tasks. A confident child will generally manage his or her feelings and make adjustments to new situations, asking for help from an adult or older child if needed. A range of coping strategies will be evident through the use of language or pretend play. In most cases children with a strong sense of self will be able to talk about how they are feeling, name their emotions and find acceptable ways to manage feelings that cause distress or discomfort. In music education activities are offered in such a way as to build self-confidence through play-based explorations. It is important that young children have many opportunities for open-ended, pleasurable, freely chosen, flexible music play. This helps them express their thoughts, feelings and imaginative wonderings and develop skills that enable them to communicate their expressions in ways that evoke emotional responses. Children play with sounds in a number of ways. These may be vocal or via the use of objects that can express musical elements such as pitch, tone and rhythm. Instrument play with drums, xylophones or even kitchen saucepans allows them to freely express their emotional state, while the exploration of songs or tunes that comprise simple musical structures can be enjoyed in an expressive and ritualized way. Open-ended play-based improvisation in music not only supports the developing child's

Help others share

personal confidence but also provides the environment for creative and expressive outcomes.

Children make emotional connections to music very early in life through significant adults in their lives. Trevarthen and Malloch (2002) have identified the importance of 'communicative musicality', suggesting that such communication between adults and young children provides the foundations for many aspects of human development and is a way of interacting that supports the regulation of young children's emotional states and behaviours. For example, the singing of lullabies can pacify and soothe a distressed child while the use of musical games can catch a young child's attention and facilitate empathy with mood or emotions. Children quickly learn to interpret the inherent qualities of a range of musical scores. Parents and teachers can create musically rich play environments in which they support creative explorations and stimulate expressive and divergent thinking about the way music makes people feel. Music that represents emotions such as happiness, sadness, anger and fear or feelings of isolation or relaxation can be used as a stimulus to discuss the nature of emotion and ways of managing feelings constructively. Such explorations provide opportunities for the extension and enrichment of emotional language and the language of coping. Moreover, there can be nothing more pleasurable or helpful to the development of self-esteem than an old fashioned 'jam session' where the young child is given the freedom to 'play out' feelings, thoughts and ideas.

Responsibility for self and others: exploration through music

As young children mature, their social skills develop significantly and by the ages of 4 and 5 they are moving beyond the primary caregiver relationship and developing a desire to interact with peers. An understanding of the social order or social rules is developed and social skill development occurs in the context of relationship building and interacting with others, most commonly through play. Extensive research indicates that play supports the 'development of self-awareness, a sense of control over the environment, verbal skill, emotional awareness, a sensitivity to the social roles they are expected to play, and the ability to explore new situations' (Skewes and Thompson, 1998, p. 36). Learning to be part of a group and developing skills such as making eye contact, taking turns, listening, empathizing, initiating and waiting become integral to the establishment of an effective social skill behaviour set. Music is an ideal tool for the development of social skills. It stimulates successful group participation, encourages positive emotional arousal and promotes the development of group membership skills. Group music offers children an opportunity to interact positively with their peers. In doing so they develop the capacity to understand class rules, take turns, model positive teacher and peer behaviours, show sensitivity to others and demonstrate an ability to plan and organize their actions. These skills are all indicators of well-developed self-control or self-regulation skills. Group music classes offer a number of activities that help support the development of self-control. These might include asking children to start and stop in time with music or sounds, taking turns playing instruments or listening and responding to the ideas of others on how a piece of music makes them feel.

Prosocial behaviour: developing through music

A young child demonstrating prosocial behaviour displays a capacity to genuinely recognize and show empathy for the feelings of others. Such behaviour calls on a higher level of moral development, a growing understanding of the ethical dimensions of relationships and a capacity to consistently cooperate, share, compromise and adhere to group rules. Once such skills are in place young children are more likely to make friends easily, recognize the needs and feelings of their friends and family, play harmoniously with peers and have the skills to solve conflicts and disagreements. Group music provides opportunities for open-ended improvisation, which encourages inventiveness, spontaneity and resourceful creative play. It also allows for structured activities, such as group singing or music making, guided discussions, cooperative movement responses, listening and generally connecting with others non-verbally and responding to the ideas of others. Group sessions typically integrate a variety of techniques, including individual or group improvisation, structured singing and listening, all of which aim for cognitive, physical, social and emotional outcomes. Class structure can often include a time for individual free improvisation where individuals have a chance to play for their friends in a 'trusted performance' segment. During this time the group sits together in a designated space, with all children being given the opportunity to perform either solos, duets or trio performances for their friends and teachers. This helps develop a range of skills, such as listening to the playing or singing of others, respecting the creative communications of others via attentive watching and focused responding and having the confidence to present personalized musical scores to an audience.

Exemplars

Linking sound making to emotion

It is a good idea not to limit the use of music to the traditional diatonic scale. Music involves the shaping and moulding of sound (any sound) to provide aesthetic experience. A strong relationship exists between feelings, movement, sound and music, and teachers and parents can easily work through a wide range of emotions, with a simple approach that requires little more than the use of the voice. For example:

Let's think of all the sounds we can and try them out:

How do we feel when we are:

- humming
- laughing
- groaning
- shouting
- whispering
- crying
- spluttering
- gasping
- snickering
- shrieking
- sighing

Complain of pain

Try to feel the quality of the sound, put your whole body behind it, how does it make you feel? Being given permission to make sounds is very exciting for young children and they easily become very absorbed in the activity. The sound of a room full of children shouting at the top of their voices may be somewhat disconcerting, but it is nonetheless a worthwhile creative experience that can be followed by a reflective discussion that focuses children's attention on the relationship of sound to emotion.

Speech sounds can also be introduced, with children being given the chance to thoroughly explore the sound and movement feeling of vowel sounds such as:

ah . . .

oh . . .

ee . . .

oo . . .

ow . . .

ai . . .

uh . . .

These sounds, along with consonants, can be correlated to the feeling states that are being explored.

Making sounds with hands and feet

Children are always willing participants in the use of hands and feet as instruments. Improvising freely with sounds made by hands clapping, fingers clicking, feet stamping and tiptoeing gives children the opportunity to feel the quality of the emotion by hearing the sound and feeling the movement in the body. For example, short, sharp, strong sounds made by clapping or stamping can be a way for children to experience what it feels like to be angry in a controlled situation.

Making music with instruments

A wide range of instruments can be used for creative expression through joint and individual music making. Steinberg (2009) reports on the value of musical play for the regulation of children's behaviour and emotional states. Musical instruments are tangible, concrete objects for young children, which can be used to cater for individual needs and learning preferences. The attraction of hand-held or 'found' instruments has been understood by early childhood educators for many years, and instruments such as:

- drums
- tambours
- tambourines
- xylophones
- bells
- tapping sticks
- triangles
- plastic containers
- stones
- pencils

are easy to handle and can be used to enhance creative expression. Through open-ended rhythmic improvisation children can be given the opportunity to explore the unique sound qualities of the instruments. As some instruments can express the quality of certain emotions or feelings better than others, teachers and parents have a role to play in their selection.

For example, bongo drums can provide an outlet for strongly felt emotion, while a xylophone offers a more relaxed and meditative experience. Explorations of rhythmic patterns allow children to use their personal energy to express inner felt emotions. At the same time such explorations enable them to draw on personally generated self-regulatory behaviours such as monitoring and modifying emotional reactions to accomplish their own goals (Denham, 1986). As Mettler (1979, p. 399) states: 'every rhythmic pattern expresses some feeling within us, although the feeling is not necessarily one which can be put into words. Rhythmic feelings are too deeply rooted physically and psychologically, and too much part of the creative core of our being to be easily verbalized'.

Musical play and the coping images

Young children learn through active experiential processing; the senses work together to provide the material for creative expression and to allow for transformation into the world of deeply felt emotion. Linking the use of the coping images to artistic modalities allows for an integrated and holistic experience and parents and teachers can use a number of different strategies to add a musical dimension to the visual stimuli provided by the images. The images lend themselves to being interpreted musically as given in the following examples:

- The 'Saying goodbye' image can be married with a simple, well-known musical score that has a repetitive and rhyming text such as, 'this is the way we wave goodbye, this is the way we wave goodbye . . .' The experience can be extended into a piece of musical theatre with the addition of gestures and clapping. Parents and teachers can use this approach, adapting many traditional children's songs or chants to work through the situations depicted in the picture and adapting the singing style to respond to the emotion or energy represented in the pictures. Taking such an approach enables children to be fully and positively involved with a situation that may be causing distress.
- The 'Scared of the dark' image can be interpreted more deeply with the addition of sound effects created by a range of vocal sounds, everyday objects or by using musical instruments. Children can be asked to identify sounds that match the emotion depicted in the picture.

Stay calm and quiet

- The 'Wanting to belong to a group' and the 'Choosing between friends' images can be used as stimuli for understanding the way different sounds work to interpret the emotional responses that these situations elicit. Parents and teachers can use the semiotic codes of music to link with the emotion applicable to the situation. A slower tempo or sad, lilting voice might be used to express the feeling of being left out of a group, while tempo variations can create suspense or tension when working through the feelings associated with having to choose between friends. Children can also be asked to create their own sound or musical scores as a way of adding to a dramatic re-enactment of a situation.
- Any of the images can be interpreted with the creation of a soundscape. Children can choose instruments to create an open improvisation (or a cacophony of sounds) to communicate the felt emotion. Giving children a chance to select the instruments and create the soundscape offers an insight into their ideas and emotional responses to the situation. As their confidence with the instruments grows, children can be given the opportunity to perform their improvisations for their peers and teachers. Parents may even wish to make audio recordings of the resultant musical scores as a way of extending the experience. Replaying the piece

of music to the children provides opportunities for deeper reflection and further individual or group discussion. Such an approach supports the development of creative problem-solving skills and provides further insight into understanding children's thinking.

Other ways in

Listening to recorded music that has been selected for its dynamic qualities and its capacity to represent a particular mood or emotion is another way parents and teachers can use music to support the use of the coping images. Listening to music is a fundamental experience for young children. For most this occurs very early in life, allowing for the processing of personal thoughts and feelings. Listening to music in a group is also a powerful experience; one that significantly supports individual verbal and social participation and encourages positive emotional arousal. Parents and teachers can use selected recorded music to facilitate 'guided listening' and to initiate conversations with children about what they are hearing and how it makes them feel. It is also appropriate for parents or teachers to talk to children about the chosen music, who wrote it, what instruments were used and the intentions of the composer in communicating a heartfelt emotion. Many well-known classical composers such as Vivaldi, Beethoven, Mozart and Camille Saint-Saen provide wide ranging musical scores that allow for both verbal and non-verbal participation.

Final thoughts

The musical experience provides children with opportunities to be creative, inventive and spontaneous and stimulates emotional responses that have a positive impact on growth and development. By taking a musical approach to interpreting the coping images we encourage positive adult–child and child–child interactions in situations that may be causing distress. Parents and teachers can try this approach to give young children an opportunity to learn how emotions can be experienced in a musical context. This encourages problem solving, active exploration, social interaction and creative meaning making.

Literacy, Language, Words and Coping: Encouraging Social and Emotional Development through Narrative

Our school has a writer's club that incorporates children across the years. Our youngest members are only 5 years old and the group is like a family, or even better – it's a gathering of all of my favourite people, a place where every single member is equally respected, included and cherished. To me, it's magical – a place where people come together to discuss all things books and write! Words simply make me feel happy and it makes the younger children feel happy too. *Hayley, 12 years, reflecting on the younger members of Writer's Club*

Rationale

Language and Literacy may be used as a vehicle for teaching coping skills, or be a strategy for coping within their own right. By acknowledging the place of social and emotional development within the language curriculum we create an opportunity for children to experience practical and helpful applications of social learning relevant to the context of their own lives.

Setting the scene

Young children clearly relish the experiences provided by an early years curriculum. They and their teachers create, sing, dance, play, write and listen to stories and an affinity for books and words is developed through this period. Children experiment with word play, rhyme, song (Pramling, 2009), take home books and listen intently when somebody reads to them. There is a natural relationship between the language curriculum and coping in the early years. Language, in all of its manifestations can have a soothing effect and function as a relaxing diversion to help young children cope with stressors in their daily lives. Nicholson and Pearson (2003) believe that the enjoyment of literacy enables children to experience an emotional release, tap into their own creativity and temporarily suspend reality.

While language and literacy may be important in their own right they provide a vehicle for teaching coping skills to children individually and in groups. As Baghban (2007) points out classroom literacy materials that are relevant to the social world of individual children not only generate interest and enthusiasm for learning but also provide valuable educational opportunities for a child's social and emotional learning. Language has been applied by educational professionals to help children cope with a wide variety of issues such as immigration (Baghban, 2000), fear (Trousdale, 1989) and stress and crisis during war (Berger and Lahad, 2010). Gonzalez (2001) says that 'we must never underestimate the power of stories in our educational processes: stories of self and stories of others . . . stories have a history behind them, are embedded in contradictions and struggle and interrogate our assumptions about the shared quality and boundaries of human groups' (p. 187).

A case study

Jamie is a 5-year-old girl in her preparatory year. Like many children of her age, Jamie loves school. She exhibits favourable attitudes towards her teacher and says her favourite activity at school is reading. Jamie is a

Cry

capable child and her teacher reports that her behaviour in the classroom is exceptional. She is engaged, independent and has good relationships with her school peers. During recess, Jamie plays with a small group of girls and, aside from the occasional bout of age-appropriate conflict, no social issues have ever been reported. However, despite the teacher's glowing observations, Jamie's mother sees a vastly different side of her daughter's behaviour when she is at home. When Jamie arrives home in the evening, her mother is often faced with tears, screams and fights. When Jamie is at home and things do not go her way, she does not seem to cope.

How can a child's ability to cope vary so markedly across different settings? Behaviour management, environmental factors at home, possible triggers or antecedents and diet can all play a part, but it is Jamie's answer to one question in particular that illuminates our inquiry. When she is asked 'is hitting the right or wrong thing to do?' Jamie answers appropriately in declaring it to be wrong. When asked the reason why, however, Jamie answers without hesitation 'because you get into trouble'. Her answer highlights a fundamental issue with the way current educational systems teach children to engage in appropriate conduct and civility towards one another. When adults employ behaviour management strategies devoid

Blame others

of social and emotional teaching, symptoms of the disruptive behaviour and not the cause is treated. Adults have learnt that actions have consequences that are not confined to punishment that, for example, harming others may result in emotional and social consequences.

In busy educational settings with jam-packed curriculums, schools can overlook social and emotional learning. This means that children can miss out on valuable lessons in social relations and coping. Social and emotional learning need not be a separate curriculum. In fact, coping skills and dialogue can be incorporated into most curricular activities. Some children do not acquire such skills incidentally. Incorporating coping dialogue in daily school life helps expose them to a rich, well-rounded education. The remainder of this chapter will outline ways in which coping skill acquisition may be facilitated by the language curriculum.

Exemplars

Create a coping story

Coping stories can be created using the coping images as a prompt for particular scenarios that young children may face in their day-to-day lives. These stories are often more effective when designed around real-life situations and issues. If a child loses a pet, for example, a coping story could be developed to facilitate strategies for the young person to use as part of coping with his or her grief and loss.

Coping stories explore the productive and non-productive strategies an individual may be using already, and draw on the reasons for the success or failure of these strategies. To make them specific, it is important to discuss the thinking, feeling and doing aspects of the coping strategy being employed, that is, what others think, feel and do in response to the strategy in question. Likewise, it is important for the child to explore the same questions in any given coping scenario or response. Using such an approach lends itself to a cognitive behavioural framework which has been demonstrated to be an efficacious way in which young children may acquire coping skills (e.g. Bailey, 2000; Graham, 1998).

Coping stories can be based around the language acquisition of the child, be made age appropriate and accommodate a vast range of learning needs. Baghban (2007) demonstrated that stories related to a child's social experiences engage interest and cultivate learning. Coping stories enable young readers to learn that stories can be about them and that their experiences are worthy of being documented in book form (Hade, 2002). An example is outlined below. Words used as sentence starters are indicated in bold typeface.

Example

My Name is Alex and I am in Grade 2 at Seymour College.
My favourite things are lunch times, early minutes and basketball.
I dislike losing things and Brussels sprouts.
My problem is that Ziggy my cat is dead. He died in the backyard. I love him and feel sad.
I coped by:

1. Crying really loud. My mum said I should have an ice cream but it did not make me feel better.
2. I had a funeral for Ziggy and I still felt sad.
3. I prayed for Ziggy.
4. I had a fight with my sister.
5. I talked to Mum and said another prayer.

The unhelpful ways I coped were fighting with my sister, and crying as I still felt sad.

This made the people around me feel angry and think that I was naughty.

When I cope this way people will not want to be around me.

This makes me feel bad.

The helpful ways I coped were talking to Mum and praying.

This made the people around me feel sorry for me **and think** that I needed help.

When I cope this way people will care for me.

This makes me feel loved.

I learnt that I should not yell at my sister and to use an inside voice at home.

Coping in a helpful way is cool.

As can be seen in the above coping story outline, the book can be adapted to suit the child and his or her current situation. This is one example of a narrative based around the stages in the coping process. While this one is quite structured, different approaches may also be adopted. Some of these are outlined below.

Coping images as story prompts

Children who require less guided instruction to create a coping narrative may benefit from the use of the situation and coping images as story prompts. A situation image could be used to set the scene or any relevant situation can be considered for discussion. Coping images can be spread out across a flat surface and used as prompts for ideas around which a story can be created. A story map or story guide may be used to help the story have a beginning, middle and an end. Alternatively ideas for the story could be brain-stormed (generated). Finished stories may take on a second life and be told to a peer or adult. Other ideas include the following:

- transcribing a story told verbally
- using an audio recording device to record the story
- record the story using a video camera.

Using audiovisual devices not only interests and motivates a young child, but also gives the process longevity. In this way the finished story can be shared with others, or reflected upon, discussed and revisited.

Story share

In a group, children sit on the floor in a circle. Using the situation images, each child takes turns to select a scenario and create a story based on the pictorial cues they have chosen.

Story share turn taking

This is a modified version of the previous activity. In line with the instructions above, children sit in a circle on the floor with situation images spread out before them. This time, a leader is selected to choose a scenario and create one sentence about the picture. Children then take turns around the circle, adding a sentence to create a colourful story. Such activities can be used to foster team building and group work. Coping can be demonstrated first-hand simply by creating a friendly environment in which children can learn.

Diary entries

Young children are often required to reflect on their weekend in a diary-style entry at the beginning of each week. This very common activity can be modified to enhance social and emotional learning if the children are asked to reflect upon a particular issue or problem they faced during the weekend and the ways in which they were able to overcome it.

Prompt questions may include the following:

- What problem did you encounter on the weekend?
- What were the ways you handled it?
- What did you think, feel, do?
- What did others think, feel, do?
- What would you do next time? Would you do the same thing?

Finish the ending . . .

The teacher verbally narrates a scenario featuring an issue or problem using a creative description based on fictional examples relevant to the children's lives. Children are then required to complete the end of the story – this may be done orally in front of the group or during writing time. Both helpful and unhelpful strategies should be explored. Some ideas are suggested as follows:

1. Molly is a friendly sea monster living in the ocean under a bed of seaweed and starfish. Molly loves to play with her sea friends, but sometimes she feels left out . . .
2. Robbie the crab just stepped on a beautiful shell. It belongs to his neighbour, Sally Star fish. It broke into a million pieces. Sally is going to be very upset.
3. Boo-whistle is a jelly fish and hates it when his mother drops him off at school. He feels sad and embarrassed as he does not want to cry in front of the other jelly fish.

Creating a story walk

This may involve a group of children. The teacher takes the children for a walk – preferably outdoors or in a park setting. The teacher begins by starting a story related to a fictional character who has an issue or a problem. The group stops periodically at points of interest along the walk, for example, a bush, tree or flower and at each stop a member of the group contributes to the story. Children may draw on their surrounds for inspiration.

Coping words

Students brainstorm a variety of words related to coping and then create acrostics (written lines containing the word) using related words. These can then be shared or displayed in a way that serves as a reminder in the classroom.

Some examples below are from a Year 2 classroom:

B: Be happy

R: Relax often

E: Empathize

A: Ask for help

T: Tell an adult when things go wrong

H: Help others

E: Enjoy something you love doing

Hug a toy

Or

How to Cope . . .

C: Care for others

O: Open communication

P: Polite and respectful talking

E: Empathize

Poetry

Children learn poetry-related skills from an early age and often enjoy listening to and creating poetry. In a Swedish study, teachers in preschools and primary schools introduced poetry to children aged between 2 and 8. Findings suggested that children have a natural inclination towards wordplay, spontaneous rhyming, punning and singing (Pramling, 2009). Pramling proposes that creating free-form poetry can help children develop 'emergent poetry' skills that are necessary for seeing and describing people, things and events in a poetic way. A didactical approach to introducing poetry to children was described, based on Heard's (1987) model:

1. Describe or narrate something.
2. Concentrate/reduce text to its essentials.

3. Try to 'get at' what one wishes to communicate by finding striking similes and/or metaphors (what is it like?)
4. Structure the text (Are there themes that reoccur, are developed or emphasised like a musical refrain? Does it consist of distinct parts? If so, how are these related? Can separation into verses and stanzas be used to create a pulse in the text?)
5. Can the sounds of the text be developed (could onomatopoeia be used?) (p. 347)

Pramling (2009) suggests that teachers focus on the children's speech and record what they say. Session leaders may also use drawings to encourage children to attend to small details and to describe how something appears and sounds to them and what it does.

Limericks are a specific type of poem that offers fun and enjoyment for children. Here is one example taken from a Year 1 classroom:

BOBBY

> There once was a pretty Mummy
> Whose kid would spit the dummy
> He yelled and he spat
> Hit his dog and his cat
> Until he had a pain in his tummy

Story book reflection

There are many beautifully illustrated picture story books that explore coping and social and emotional learning. Session leaders may harness these resources to teach coping by reflecting on the coping moments discussed in the book or evinced by the central characters.

Questions following such a story may include:

- What happened?
- What was the outcome?
- What did the character, think, feel, do?
- How did other characters in the book think, feel, do?
- What could the character have done differently?
- How would this have changed the outcome?
- How would this have changed what the character and others thought, felt and did as a result?

Interactions: an observation of coping images in practice

Interaction 1: Making a choice

The teacher presented a line drawing to the children of a small child having to choose between two groups of friends.

Age of children: 3–4 years

Session type: Group time, storytelling

Teacher instruction: What do you see?

Examples of responses from children:

'The little boy is thinking who[m] to play with.'

'The boy is deciding whether to play with the ball or the tea set.'

'The boy is choosing to play with the boys or the girls'

Teacher instruction: What do you think?

'I think he can't decide.'

'I think he might be choosing to play with the boys because he is a boy.'

'Boys can play with girls too. I play with girls.'

'May be the girls don't want to play with the boys.'

Teacher instruction: What do you feel?

'Sometimes I don't know who to play with.'

Sometimes I want to play with some children but they don't want to play with me.'

'I think he cannot decide, and he is a bit sad.'

Teacher instruction: What do you do?

'I will go and play with the boys first, then go and play with the girls.'

'May be they can all play together.'

'Sometimes you choose where your best friend is playing too. But friends don't have to play together all the time.'

Teacher's creative approach (from teacher's comments) The group talked about what factors to consider in making a choice – making 'safe choices', 'wise choices' and 'kind choices'. This was a follow-up of the discussion they had about 'gentle hands, 'helpful hands' and 'wise hands'. The coping image and situation image are displayed in the room for further discussion about

⇨

making 'safe', 'wise' and 'kind' choices in response to children's recent 'unwise' choices and 'unsafe' choices made during play.

What would you like to do next?

The teacher reported that future sessions will discuss more about gender issue in making a choice in play, which children seem to suggest quite consistently in the discussion.

Interaction 2: Teasing

Age of children: 4–5 years

Session type: Group discussion, storytelling

Keep feelings private

Teacher instruction: What do you see?
'One boy is all alone and the other boys are being mean to him.'
'The big boys are being nice to the little boy.'

Teacher instruction: What do you think?
'The big boys are being mean to the other boys and that is not nice.'

Teacher instruction: What do you feel?
`the boy feels sad"
`the boy is scared"
`and cross'

From general discussion: Teacher instruction: What do you do?
Examples of responses from children
'Tell the teachers.'
'Tell mum and dad.'
'Ask the big boy nicely to get the toy back. Like saying please.'

Teacher's comments: The group looked at the coping images and children agreed that 'talk to an adult' is the most appropriate for coping with this situation. Children said they will 'cry' because they will be sad. They also suggested they will 'hug a toy'.

Teacher's creative approach: The group discussed about why 'talk to an adult' is particularly important in coping with this situation and that 'keeping your feelings to self' is not a good idea. Children emphasis that 'hugging a toy' and 'cry might make you feel better after feeling sad, and they also suggested that 'thinking about happy thoughts' and 'play' will make them happy again after being teased. Teacher also shared a few other examples of 'teasing' scenarios with the children.

Other ways in

Questions can help children identify and draw from the coping strategies used by characters in story books. Some questions may help children relate the character's experiences to their own. Disque and Langenbrunner (1996) provide a list of questions to help children identify with the story:

- What are some of the things you liked most about the book?
- Who would like\ to draw a picture of a favourite character?
- Who can say something or make a noise like a character?
- If you could be like one of the characters, which one would you be?
- What do you think you will remember about the story? (p. 4)

Final thoughts

Teaching children coping skills has a place within the broader curriculum, one that is not simply limited to the dramatic arts, dance and language. An analogy can be made with the solving of numerical problems. These are in essence no different to the types of problems people face day-to-day; however, most people are more inclined to calmly and carefully consider options and solutions and work towards solutions to numerical problems. The skills that are developed in this area provide a good understanding of the way people cope with the wider world.

Developing Coping Skills in the Family Context: Harnessing the Strengths of a Family Group to Create Positive Outcomes for Young People

It is better to ask for help from Mum or Dad than to get angry because you can hurt people's feelings. I also like to have a cuddle or go outside. When I am scared, I yell out 'Daddy!' I might also cuddle a teddy or climb into his bed. *Norah, 7 years*

Rationale

Exposure to significant others during a child's early years enables young children to observe how others cope when confronted with daily hassles and concerns. Parents and families serve as important role models in a young person's life and important social learning takes place at home and in the family context. Many of the activities suggested throughout the volume can be used in a family context, particularly those included in Chapter 8, Literacy, Language, Words and Coping.

Setting the scene

In 1977, a researcher leaned over a 12-day-old baby, stuck out his tongue, pursed his lips, stood back and observed the infant's reaction. Moments later the infant copied him (Meltzoff and Moore, 1977). Learning begins at birth and extends well into old age and the family plays a significant role in this journey. As the classic psychology experiment demonstrated, a child begins to interact within a social context almost from the moment he or she is born. These early interactions are shaped by the family environment and it is during these formative years that a child learns to navigate the world in which he or she belongs. Parent characteristics and practices are a clear influence on children's self-regulation and developmental outcomes. For example, parents' expressiveness, and in particular their use of negative emotions, is a predictor for children's adaptation (Liew et al., 2003; Valiente et al., 2004).

Parent influences

Socialization from parents and care givers has an important influence on children's coping processes, and therefore adjustment, in three ways: through coaching, modelling, and context (Kliewer et al., 2006). Coaching refers to direct suggestions caregivers make regarding how to think about (appraise) or respond to (cope with) a situation. For example, a caregiver might suggest that a situation is not as bad as a child thinks because of resources available to the child, or a caregiver might recommend a particular course of action that the child could take (e.g. come talk to me; think through what you could do). Modelling refers to caregiver appraisals and coping behaviours that are observed by the child. For example, a caregiver may routinely catastrophize a situation or may model support-seeking coping behaviours. Context refers to the environmental background against which

Broken toy

coping behaviors are learned, enacted, and reinforced, encompassing both the caregiver – child relationship and broader family interaction patterns' (pp. 605–6).

How children are taught to cope (both actively and proactively) with day-to-day events and stressors inform their ability to cope later in life (Aldwin et al., 2010). Notwithstanding the importance of these early childhood experiences and lessons, coping is a lifelong skill that continues to develop both within and external to the family throughout our lives. This chapter examines how a child's ability to cope is influenced by family life. It discusses common family stressors, as well as strategies and suggestions for ways in which families can contribute positively to the coping skill acquisition and resiliency of young children.

Parents are hugely influential in shaping a child's ability to cope (e.g. Eisenberg et al., 1998) and Peterson and Leigh (1990) have found that, even when attempting to control their influence, parents unintentionally model behaviours in their day-to-day lives. Social learning theory (Bandura, 1977; Bandura and Walters, 1963) suggests that children learn through observation, mediated by vicarious reinforcement, that is, observing the rewards (reinforcements) and consequences experienced by others. Young children evaluate situations based on their own perceptions of possible intrinsic or extrinsic reinforcement (e.g. approval by self or approval by others) and envisaging the possible consequences of their actions. Children 'observe the actions of others, acquire information, and develop expectancies that guide their own actions and internal standards in subsequent situations' (Peterson and Leigh, 1990, p. 120). This is relevant to contemporary understanding of the ways in which children perceive the coping strategies employed by their parents or other significant adults in their lives.

It is clear that parents' behaviour serves as a model for the coping behaviour of young children. Parents who employ productive coping solutions to day-to-day issues are likely to be positive role models for their young children. Parents who adopt passive or rigid processes to cope with a problem are not ideal role models, nor are they able to provide the best support for the development of a young child's productive coping repertoire (Shulman, 1993). Studies show that the ideal role model for a young child learning successful coping (Chacko et al., 2009; Eisenberg et al., 1998; Garner and Estep, 2001):

- is able to effectively communicate emotions
- is able to provide a nurturing and supportive environment
- allows the child to express his or her feelings and ideas
- articulates the benefits of responding to an issue in a positive way
- can express concerns about likely consequences
- actively teaches coping skills.

Stresses in the family

The experience of divorce and separation of parents is a major stress for many young children. Between a third to a half of all relationships end in divorce or separation in Western countries such as Australia, the United States and the United Kingdom.

Emery (1988) points out that,

> In considering how children cope with divorce, the difficulties typically involved in adaptation should not be minimised, whilst the frequency with which family transition leads to abnormal outcomes must not be overstated . . .

Worry

divorce has become a very common event . . . to suggest its impact on children is inevitably pathological is an injustice to a large number of families. To suggest that divorce is an insignificant transition reveals insensitivity. (p. 11)

While divorce does not invariably have negative effects (Emery, 1988; Hauser and Bowlds, 1990), parental separation elicits a range of coping responses and outcomes for children. There are some young people whose age and ability-related development continues apace, regardless of family circumstance, while others experience long-term effects. Young children may blame themselves, externalize their behaviours and act out (Wallerstein and Lewis, 2004). Commonly, children will look towards their parents for coping strategies and attempt to either adopt or mirror the reactions of the significant adults around them. Young children may often even endeavour to play a support role themselves.

A number of children were interviewed over a six-month period to evaluate common stressors affecting them within the family context. The following is a list of the key findings related to the perceived stressors of young children as reported by the cohort interviewed.

- Death of a pet
- Separation of parents
- Being reprimanded by an adult
- Conflict with sibling

Fears and stressors change as a child develops (see Chapter 2, Stress, Concerns and Coping). One group of researchers (Robinson and Rotter, 1991) found that the most common fears in early childhood were related to:

- strangers
- separation of parent
- dark rooms
- large animals
- mystical creatures

What families can do to develop helpful coping skills?

Families play a vital role in nurturing and encouraging coping skills. Educators should be encouraged to provide families with the necessary information to help young children adapt the coping skills they are learning at school to the home environment.

Conversations about coping may take place in educational settings through activities and materials such as:

- information evenings
- workshops
- newsletter articles
- homework activities
- information sheets
- parent teacher interviews.

The remainder of this chapter will outline ways in which families may engage with young children to enhance their social and emotional learning opportunities. These activities, which reflect those that may also take place in the classroom, offer an opportunity for parents, caregivers, siblings or other relations to help young children adopt a holistic approach to learning such skills in a home setting.

Exemplars

Coping using a problem-solving model

The family context is an ideal environment for teaching problem solving. While problem-solving skills are acquired continually throughout a lifetime, there is evidence to suggest they can be taught in the early years. Every day situations, which present themselves in the home, afford families various opportunities for adopting the model. Problem solving may be accomplished in six steps. Younger children who require prompting may benefit from observing significant adults applying these steps as issues and problems arise.

Step 1. Using a set of coping images, a child or family member should select one scenario image to work on at a time. The child could be asked to identify the following: (a) What is happening in the picture? (b) How is everyone feeling? (c) What is everyone thinking? Children might be asked to seek clues from subtleties in the picture (e.g. facial expressions, body language).

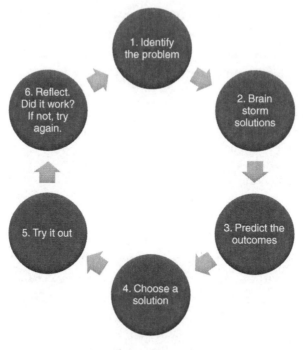

Steps for problem solving

Step 2. The family member then asks the child to brainstorm solutions using the coping (solution) images. Children should be encouraged to pick all possible solutions, not just those they feel are the *correct* answers. All the images can be placed on the table, or only those that are appropriate to the situation can be put out.

Step 3. The child is then asked to predict the outcome of each of the solutions chosen. The child must identify the following: (a) What will happen? (b) How he or she would feel in the situation? (c) How others would feel in the situation? (d) What others may think as a result of the situation?

Step 4. The child is asked to pick the most desirable solution. The child may be asked to explain why this solution was chosen over the others.

Step 5. If the scenario is based on one the child is experiencing in real life, he or she could be asked to *try out* the chosen solution. Alternatively, the child could be asked to role-play or act out the desirable scenario/solution pair and compare it with a less desirable solution in order to consolidate an understanding of the problem-solving process. The family can often provide the opportunity for role-play as various members can be assigned 'roles', or alternatively become audience members.

Step 6. This final step only applies if the scenario/solution is one the child has attempted to *try out* in real life. The child is asked to reflect on whether or not the solution worked for his or her situation. The child could be asked the following: (a) What happened? (b) Did this fix the problem? What was the outcome? How did the people involved feel? What do you think they thought? (c) Would you try it again next time? (d) Is there a better solution available? If yes, what would you try next time?

Developing a coping vocabulary

With typically developing children, adults often attach labels and vocabulary to new skills as the young child acquires them. For example, when a child learns to walk, the word *walking* is automatically used to describe the new skill acquisition – this helps provide reinforcement for the skill, that is, 'great walking', as well as corrective feedback, that is, 'whoopsy daisy, fell over. Up again'. The labelling of behaviour associated with a skill helps a child with further learning, consolidation, generalization and mastery; providing labels is as much a part of learning as it is of teaching. When teaching coping skills, vocabulary is equally important. As coping skills are often learnt incidentally, vicariously or through observation (as opposed to being taught explicitly like reading or writing), professionals can sometimes neglect to label the specific behaviours associated with coping. For those wishing to teach a child adaptive coping behaviours to replace frequently occurring maladaptive ones, labelling is an important way of developing goals. It provides feedback – either praise for effort or consequence – and ensures consistency in the approach of all those who spend time with the child.

Coping images can be used to increase a child's coping vocabulary in a variety of ways. Traditional games can be a helpful way of presenting the images in a fun fashion:

- **Memory**: two sets of coping images are required. The images are shuffled and placed face down on the table. Adult and child take turns to flip two images, naming each image they turn. If the images are not a pair they are placed face down where they were found. If the images are a pair they are collected and the player has another turn. The player with the most pairs at the end of the game wins. Memory games are a useful way of exposing children to the language of coping.

- **Flash cards**: coping images may be used as flashcards and presented to the child so that he or she can verbally name the coping strategy displayed.
- **Snap**: two sets of coping images are required to play snap. The images can be made into a deck of cards which can then be shuffled, split in two and placed face down in front of each player. The adult and the child take turns to reveal one card at a time to form a new pile. Players must name each card they turn over. When two matching cards are placed on top of each other, players must place their hand on the deck and call 'snap'. The player whose hand reaches the deck first collects the cards. The winner is the person who has the most cards.
- **Charades**: coping images/cards are placed into a container. Players take turns to choose a coping image and act it out so that the other player can guess which coping strategy is being performed.
- **Colouring activity**: coping images may be photocopied in grey scale and used for a colouring activity. The child can describe the coping strategies pictured while colouring in the line drawing.
- **Fish**: attach a paper clip to each coping image/card and face them upside down on the floor. Using a magnet attached to a piece of string, the child picks up each of the coping images. As each image is lifted, the child is required to name the image selected.

Coping images for fun and games

Families should endeavour to find new and interesting ways to keep the development of coping skills fun and interesting. It is important to maintain the interest of the child and foster rapport. To this end families sometimes need to exercise their inner creativity:

- **Coping dash**: Coping images are stuck to the wall using a removable adhesive. The coping images should be spaced out evenly along a reasonably sized wall at the child's height. The adult reads out each scenario one at a time and the child is expected to dash between the appropriate coping responses as fast as possible. The adult can alter the speed with which the scenarios are read to create excitement!
- **Coping quick fingers**: Coping images are spread out face up across a large floor area. The adult sets a kitchen timer to 10 seconds (this can vary depending on the ability of the child), and reads out a scenario. The child is then required to find appropriate coping responses within the time limit. The time allowance may be

varied to create interest. The child could be given points for selecting cards within the time limit. To encourage responsibility and
maintain interest, the child and the adult may switch roles so that
the adult is now required to find responses within a time limit.

Interactions: an observation of coping images in practice

Interaction 1: Separation from parent

Age of children: 3–4 years
Session type: Parent and child or teacher led group discussion

Worry leaving

Parent/teacher instruction: What do you see?
'The boy is going to school and the boy is waving goodbye.'
'The mummy is dropping the children at school and saying
goodbye.'

⇨

'The boy is saying goodbye to mummy at kinder.'
Parent/teacher instruction: What do you think?
'I think the little boy is a bit worried that his mummy is not coming with him.'
'I think he is sad because he doesn't know where to go.'
'Maybe he is sad because he doesn't know anyone at kinder.'
Child M: 'I think he is sad to say goodbye to mummy. He wants to stay with mummy.'
Parent/teacher instruction: What do you feel?
'I'm sad when I come to kinder sometimes, not because I don't like to come to kinder, I just want to stay with mum and dad.'
Child M: 'All I want is to go home with mummy. I'm sad.'
Parent/teacher instruction: What do you do?
'Cry and scream; hug a toy; play; talk to teacher.'
Child M: 'I will cry and cry until mummy comes back. I don't know what time mummy is coming back.'
Parent/teacher's creative approach: Teachers have placed the situation image and the coping images on display in the room, and have encouraged those children with separation difficulties to look at and talk about the coping images with their parents at drop-off in the morning and talk about what he/she is going to do after mum and dad leave. Teachers reported them as being very useful.

Final thoughts

The use of coping images is not limited to any specific method. There are a number of ways they may be used within a familial context, with variety and fun being the key to success. The coping images may be used by families in ways demonstrated above or, as one parent suggested, 'they can be used as a good starting point for conversations.' Other suggestions include – storytelling, creating poems, songs and drawings – ideas for which may be drawn from other chapters in this book.

The function and use of coping images can change depending on the need, preference and ability of each child. What may be developmentally appropriate for a 4 year old, may not be so for an 8 year old. Therefore, it is important to demonstrate a general understanding of the age appropriateness of the games adopted.

Talk to an adult

The family is the cradle where young children are nurtured, cushioned and buttressed in the course of their development; it is the place that generally provides a most ready access to social support. Families vicariously facilitate coping in young children by creating a natural place for social support and safety (Bradley 2007). The ongoing challenge for individuals working in educational settings is to create safe and effective means by which families can be involved in the social and emotional learning of their young children. A holistic approach extending from the classroom to the family home provides a greater opportunity for children to thrive and develop and acquire the resourcefulness to help them to cope with whatever comes their way.

Coping and Clinical Contexts: Supporting a Child Working with an External Health Professional

10

Coping is important because it helps your emotions. Coping can be asking someone to give you a band-aid when you fall over. Sarah (psychologist) helps me to say nice words and helps me to do kind things. She thinks I'm excellent and helps with things that happen during the week. Seeing her is very cool. *Kayla, 11 years*

Rationale

Despite interventions, strategies and environmental considerations operating within the school to help children learn social and emotional skills, there are times when their difficulties persist and they are referred to an external professional for specialized intervention. This chapter outlines ways in which educational professionals can assist in identifying children who may require additional help, as well support those children once they are engaged in external intervention. Clinicians perspectives are also presented.

Setting the scene

Some educational settings prioritize the implementation of activities and strategies to enhance coping skills during early childhood. Some of these activities may be a part of a wider whole-school framework, others may be embedded in the curriculum, while some are one-off sessions held within the classroom as the need arises. A common question from educators concerns those children who do not respond to the social and emotional learning opportunities provided in the school context. Often, despite having the opportunity to participate in such activities and to experience the positive and proactive coping skills of others, some children continue to exhibit aberrant coping patterns when dealing with daily challenges. Various factors come into play including age, emotional maturity, behaviour triggers, management of behavioural consequences, how the child presents in different contexts (e.g. home, school, in other people's houses) and recent events. If the disruptive behaviour continues despite intervention, educational professionals often wonder when to refer the issue to a psychologist or allied health professional. Some children do not acquire coping skills incidentally or in the classroom. In these cases, coping skills may need to be taught in a clinical context by a suitably qualified professional, where learning can be based on individual needs. This chapter explores the empirical evidence for teaching coping skills within a clinical context and considers when and why a psychologist or allied health professional may be helpful. When an external professional is involved with a young child it is important that all significant adults in the child's life adopt a consistent approach. The following deals with some strategies that enable educational professionals to best help a young child undergoing support in a clinical context.

Differentiation

Children with pervasive developmental disorders such as autism or Asperger's syndrome may benefit from interventions that explicitly teach coping strategies (Brookman-Frazee et al., 2009). Interventions that focus on teaching skills related to self-regulation, managing cognitions, identification and recognition of emotions, as well as problem solving, have been shown to be important for the social integration of these children. Bailey (2000) suggests that children with deficits in social and problem-solving skills can be taught principles of competent social behaviour through coping intervention. The interventions can be supplemented and supported by role-play, the use of videotape feedback and social stories ™ Carol Gray (2001).

Teaching coping strategies to children with other clinical diagnoses (e.g. depression, anxiety, ADHD and conduct disorder) has also been successful (Bailey, 2000; Brookman-Frazee et al., 2009).

Interventions facilitated by a clinician require children to focus on explicit skill acquisition and mastery within a clinical context, with an emphasis on generalizing the acquired skills to other environmental contexts (e.g. school and home). Practice, repetition and consistency of approach by significant adults are important when helping such children successfully integrate these skills into more naturalistic settings.

When to refer to a psychologist, counsellor, psychiatrist, social worker or related professional

Psychologists and related professionals provide assistance, support and intervention for a wide range of concerns and issues, including those pertinent to early childhood. When a young child is not responding to social and emotional learning it may be time to consider a referral to a psychologist or related professional for assessment. Similarly, a child exhibiting behaviour that is not age appropriate or who is in some way unable to access the day-to-day social and academic learning opportunities of children of the same age may require referral. The following are some of the concerns that may warrant referral to a psychologist:

- Persistent anxiety
- Overwhelming worries or fears
- School refusal
- Rigid routines and obsessions
- Fluctuations in mood
- Disruptive behaviour
- Disturbances in sleep or appetite
- Academic difficulties
- Socialization concerns
- Developmental delay
- Inability to cope with life's problems
- Mental health issues (e.g. depression, disordered eating)
- Neurological issues
- Attention difficulties
- Externalizing behaviours including bedwetting, anger or acting out
- Developmental disorders (e.g. autism)
- A significant change in mood, interests or academic ability
- Regular physical complaints (e.g. headache, stomach ache, or not feeling well).

Tantrum

Life events such as grief and loss (e.g. death of a pet), life transitions (e.g. a change in schools), pain management or illness, school concerns (e.g. bullying) or the experience of a traumatic event (e.g. physical, sexual or emotional abuse) may also warrant the intervention of an external professional.

Children who experience developmental delay in key milestone areas such as walking, talking and toilet training can also benefit from seeing a psychologist or paediatrician.

A clinician's perspective

When a clinician engages with the young person in a clinical, family or classroom setting many of the activities relating to coping offered throughout the volume can be adapted for individual or group activity. For example, where a child is having difficulty coping with separation from a parent, there is likely to be a detailed assessment of what is the underlying cause of the anxiety. Following an extensive assessment the practitioner can use the situation image such as 'Saying goodbye' and explore how the child deals with the situation by offering them a selection from the coping images that are likely to reflect current coping. It is then possible to explore more ideal ways of coping from another set of images. These images become prompts to clinical intervention.

In a similar way when there is a problem of any sort that requires clinical intervention, such as extended exposure to teasing or bullying, fear of something new, grief and loss, the clinician can make use of the images in creative ways. First, there is the possibility of using the situation images or creating a situation image that fits the circumstance. Then there is the possibility of exploring the child's emotional reaction to the situation, either verbally, through projective play or through drawing. Similarly descriptions and examples of coping can be elicited from the child. The coping can be evaluated and possibilities of use of different coping skills can be explored through any of the media that are available to the clinician, including the coping images. One universally useful tool that can be adapted for most situations is the problem-solving activity presented in Chapter 9, Developing Coping Skills in the Family Context.

Clinicians work in different ways, sometimes individually in a play setting where any of the above suggestions may be utilized, as can the numerous activities throughout the book, including those relating to the arts, including dance, music and the visual arts. The activities described in Chapter 4, Developing Coping Skills in a Universal Group, can be adapted to individuals or small clinical groups such as children referred for social anxiety. The clinician can also engage with the peer group of a referred child to problem solve. For example, when a child is not attending school because of an anxiety factor, changes can be made in numerous ways, including establishing peer group support for the anxious child.

Finally, many clinicians work in different ways with parents, sometimes including the child with the family, and sometimes as a resource for parents. The coping and situation images can be used by clinicians in a family therapy context. For example, with the family 'playing' a coping game that reflects on everybody's coping rather than that of the identified child. Alternatively, the clinician becomes a parent-coach in how to use the situation and coping images with their child or children.

There are no limits to the inventiveness of clinicians to utilize strategies for assessment and intervention as well as skill development for particular children.

The impact of positive psychology in educational settings

The positive psychology movement has resulted in a shift in the reasons why individuals, including children access a psychologist or related professional. Rather than focusing on a pathological perspective where individuals only see a psychologist in cases of illness or when things go wrong, positive psychology has emphasized the benefits of proactive and preventative intervention (Seligman and Csikszentmihalyi, 2000). The productive coping skills of most individuals can be improved, regardless of whether clinical concerns pertain. Positive psychologists propound the belief that individuals should visit a psychologist to improve a variety of aspects associated with their lives. In the early years these may include setting goals, improving academic outcomes, positive thinking, proactive coping and increasing general well-being and happiness.

How to assist a child under the care of an external professional

The generalization and transfer of skills from a clinical context into the classroom is essential for the long-term success of a young child. The following points are important to facilitate a consistent approach:

- Keep the lines of communication open. Seek permission from the parent to speak to the external professional. Ask for guidance and recommendations as there may be some strategies that could be applied in the classroom. Some teachers create a communication diary for the child so that parents, teachers and external professionals involved with the young child can communicate with each other readily.
- If concerns persist in the classroom, request that the external professional conduct an observation. An observation can be a good way to receive feedback and advice based on the specific classroom context.
- Listen to the child's feelings. Listening is not always convenient for a teacher; however, setting time aside to listen to the child can be a helpful way of seeking appropriate modes of help when required.
- Be a positive role model and discuss positive ways of dealing with difficult situations and emotions.

Supporting through the classroom

Coping images as visual helpers

The clear and specific images used on coping images enable them to be employed as *visual helpers*. Visual helpers are concrete, non-transient images that help children process information and interact successfully in their learning environment. Research suggests that 40 per cent of children learn kinaesthetically (i.e. through experience), 40 per cent visually and just 20 per cent via auditory methods. A large amount of learning in the classroom or clinical environment, however, is still presented orally. While it is difficult to present all learning material in a visual format, visual helpers can support concepts such as coping skills that some children may struggle with.

Research has demonstrated that visual aides are beneficial for children who exhibit:

- auditory processing problems
- receptive language delay
- autism spectrum disorders
- persistent disorganization
- learning difficulties
- English as a second language
- hearing impairment
- oppositional defiant disorder
- attention deficit hyperactivity disorder (ADHD/ADD)

Coping images may be used as a visual helper in a classroom context, clinical setting as well as in orchestrated activities with the whole class. Often, it is helpful to teach coping skills experientially – *in the moment.* Coping images may be displayed in the room, discussed or pointed to as a prompt for students during activities in which coping skills are being taught and targeted (as a part of an individual learning plan). Many well-known board games already available in the market can be useful in teaching coping skills. Such board games require young children to wait their turn, share, lose graciously, read social cues, communicate effectively, compromise, negotiate, resolve conflict, listen and use social-based language. An ability to cope underpins all of these skills and so specific coping images may be used to formulate targeted skills for a young person as a part of an intervention.

Visual helpers will help children who have difficulties with the following:

- listening and attending
- understanding and responding
- processing sequenced information
- motivation and play
- following instructions and routines
- anxiety and resistance to change
- social isolation and shyness
- challenging behaviours

Goal setting

Goal setting is an important aspect of working with young children, and an external professional may set goals to be carried over into the classroom. Goals help to provide a function and purpose for the intervention and can be shared with others who work with the child in order to ensure a consistency of approach. When a group of individuals in the child's life work on the same skill, it helps the child with the mastery and generalization of that skill. Goal setting can be child-directed or adult-directed, depending on the level of the child's motivation and ability. It is important for teachers to be aware of which goals are set by the external professional so that they can work towards achieving success for the child.

Irrespective of whether goals are set by an adult or the child, a token economy (i.e. a system of rewards) can be helpful in ensuring that the child remains motivated to achieve success. While many children are satisfied by the intrinsic reward that accompanies doing the right thing, some children require the motivation of extrinsic rewards to help them achieve their goals. A token board or star chart can be a helpful way of rewarding a child in such cases.

A case study

Mia is an 8-year-old girl currently living with her mother. Mia's teacher describes her as an average student who completes work tasks and is on par academically with same-age peers. Mia's teacher reports that Mia is difficult to engage with socially, a problem that appears more overt in the playground than in the classroom. Mia's mother confirms that Mia has poor social skills, which she suspects may be a function of being an only child, her preference for solitary play, and her dislike for sport or competition-based games. Mia's mother states that from an early age, Mia has disliked friends at school. Mia's teacher confirms this and reports that although Mia can identify herself as having various friends at school, she exhibits many problems, particularly at lunchtimes. Such problems include an inability to resolve conflicts with her friends, a tendency to be 'bossy' and 'controlling', and a tendency to exhibit violent and inappropriate behaviours (e.g. hitting, kicking and pinching). Both Mia's teacher and mother agree that Mia becomes frustrated easily and has difficulty managing anger. It is during such times, according to Mia's teacher, that Mia has a tendency to 'act-out'.

Mia's teacher and mother also observe poor organizational and planning skills in her daily routine. Mia requires prompting and constant verbal reminders to organize all facets of school routine, particularly with regard to those in the morning and afternoon. Mia's mother reports that if it weren't for her 'nagging' in the morning they would never arrive at school. Recently, school reports have expressed concern over Mia becoming increasingly disruptive during class time. Mia's teacher reports that Mia has occasionally been seen to verbally and physically 'bully' her classmates.

Last year, at the request of her Mother, Mia saw a paediatrician who investigated the possibility of Asperger's syndrome (AS). No diagnosis has been reported, although the paediatrician indicated that Mia exhibited 'some traits' of AS and recommended various behavioural-based interventions for managing her challenging behaviours and ongoing support from an educational psychologist.

Using coping images to teach social skills

There is an expectation that all individuals display appropriate social skills within the norms of their culture. Conforming to the often unspoken rules of sociability enables the formation and maintenance of relationships that will help individuals to be independent and successful. Social skills have been defined as a set of learned, identifiable behaviours that contribute to an individual's functioning in society (Quinn et al., 1996). Pavri and Luftig (2000) suggest that those who display inappropriate social behaviours are less appealing to their peers and have problems throughout life. For example, without adequate social skills an individual may experience problems with employment, daily living skills, independent living and connectedness to society. The difficulties that some children have with social interactions result in atypical social development that may have a devastating effect on their ability to establish positive relationships at home, at school, and in community settings.

Hidden social rules and norms are manifest in every aspect of mainstream schools (i.e. classroom, playground and bathroom) and create great difficulties for some. Some children behave in ways that are socially inappropriate and do not conform to social or group norms within mainstream educational settings. Rules surrounding acceptable and non-acceptable behaviours often need to be taught, as do social cues that inform us when others may be disapproving of our behaviour (Napier and Gershenfeld, 2004).

Social skills training provides a way for children to learn appropriate social skills in a small group that facilitates cohesive and comfortable interactions with their peers (Simpson et al., 1991). Bellini (2004) suggests that social skills are acquired through observation, modelling, coaching and social problem solving as well as rehearsal, feedback and reinforcement-based strategies. The efficacy of such social skills groups is well documented (e.g. Quinn et al., 1996). The groups that are most successful tend to focus on one social skill at a time and involve a systemically orientated approach as opposed to a *stand-alone* or pullout intervention. Research on friendship and social skill-based programmes have shown they help reduce anxiety (Barrett, 1998),

Help others

improve problem-solving skills (Day et al., 1999), promote the use of self-regulation strategies (McDonnell et al., 2001) and increase social competence (Nimmo, 1993).

The social skills group

With the assistance of an external educational psychologist, a social skills group was developed for Mia, which consisted of five other girls selected from her year level. The group was carefully selected according to the student's level of sociability based on teacher observations. A mixed-ability group aimed to provide vicarious learning opportunities, group discussions, small group/pair work and a microcosmic sample of social situations that might be faced in the playground. Coping images were used to facilitate discussions around the following topics:

- Getting to Know You
- Friendly Body
- Friendly Voice
- Friendly Listening
- Play Skills
- Feelings
- Conflict
- Compromising
- Compliments
- Helping People
- Manners.

Counselling

Specialized 1:1 social behaviour teaching was implemented for Mia to learn appropriate responses to situations. This was a reactive approach and was often conducted in the moment of a behavioural problem in the classroom or at playtime. During this time the use of coping images and other tools such as social stories, role-plays, comic strips and emotion thermometers were used to consolidate concepts. Emphasis was placed on good and bad choices, in line with the behavioural management strategies and language of the school.

Run away

Final thoughts

If concerns about a child's social skills, emotions or well-being are identified, teachers are advised to speak to senior colleague or school clinical consultant for advice in the first instance. Often schools have their own referral procedures that need to be followed. Talking about the issues at hand with parents can also be a good starting point. Parents are generally experts regarding their own child and may be a good resource for management strategies or recommendations. The involvement of parents may also create conversations, which can help shed further light on the issues of concern. It is important for teachers to provide guidance and support for parents should they wish to involve an external professional. The school psychologist is often a good starting point. Parents may also find relevant *helplines* in their area or seek out their local GP as a valuable resource.

References

Aldwin, C. M., Yancura, L. A. and Boeninger, D. K. (2010). Coping across the lifespan. In R. E. Lerner (Series Ed.) and A. M. Freund and M. E. Lamb (Vol. Eds), *Handbook of Lifespan Development*. New York: Wiley.

Ames, C. and Archer, J. (1988). Achievement goals in the classroom: students' learning strategies and motivation processes. *Journal of Education Psychology, 80,* 260–7.

Amirkhan, J. H. (1990). A factor analytically derived measure of coping: the coping strategy indicator. *Journal of Personality and Social Psychology, 59,* 1066–75.

Anvari, S. H., Trainor, L. J., Woodside, J. and Levy, B. A. (2002). Relations among musical skills, phonological processing, and early reading ability in preschool children. *Journal of Experimental Child Psychology, 83,* 111–30.

Averill, J. R. and Thomas-Knowles, C. (1991). Emotional creativity. In K. T. Strongman (Ed.), *International Review of Studies on Emotion* (Vol. 1, pp. 269–99). New York: Wiley.

Baghban, M. (2000). Conversations with Yep and Soentpiet: negotiating between cultures: establishing a multicultural identity through writing and illustrating. *Dragon Lode, 18,* 41–51.

— (2007). Immigration in childhood: using picture books to cope. *The Social Studies,* March–April.

Bailey, V. (2000). Cognitive-behavioural therapies for children and adolescents. *Advances in Psychiatric Treatment, 7,* 224–32.

Band, E. and Weisz, J. (1988). How to feel better when it feels bad: children's perspectives on coping with everyday stress. *Developmental Psychology, 24,* 247–53.

Bandura, A. (1977). *Self-Efficacy: The Exercise of Control.* New York: W. H. Freeman.

Bandura, A. and Walters, R. (1963). *Social Learning and Personality Development.* New York: Holt, Rinehart & Winston.

Barrett, M. S. (2005). Musical communication and children's communities of musical practice. In D. Miell, R. MacDonald and D. Hargreaves (Eds), *Musical Communication* (pp. 261–80). Oxford: Oxford University Press.

Barrett, P. M. (1998). An evaluation of cognitive-behavioural group treatments for childhood anxiety disorders. *Journal of Clinical Child Psychology, 64,* 333–42.

Bauer, D. H. (1976). An exploratory study of developmental changes in children's fears. *Journal of Child Psychology and Psychiatry, 17,* 69–74.

Bellini, S. (2004). Social skill deficits and anxiety in high functioning adolescents with autism spectrum disorders. *Focus on Autism and Other Developmental Disabilities, 19,* 78–86.

Berger, R. and Lahad, M. (2010). A safe place: ways in which nature, play and creativity can help children cope with stress and crisis – establishing the kindergarten as a safe haven where children can develop resiliency. *Early Child Development and Care, 180,* 889–900.

Betensky, M. (1995). *What Do You See? Phenomenology of Therapeutic Art Expression*. London: Jessica Kingsley.

Blechman, E. A., Prinz, R. J. and Dumas, E. J. (1995). Coping, competence, and aggression prevention. Part 1: Developmental Model. *Applied and Preventive Psychology*, *4*, 211–32.

Boorman, J. (1969). *Creative Dance in the First Three Grades*. New York: D. McKay.

— (1973). *Dance and Language Experiences with Children*. Don Mills, ON: Academic Press Canada.

Bradley, R. H. (2007). Parenting in the breach: how parents help children cope with developmentally challenging circumstances. *Parenting: Science and Practice*, *7*, 99–148.

Brookman-Frazee, L., Vismara, Drahota, A., Stahmer, A. and Openden, D. (2009). Parent training interventions for children with Autism spectrum disorders. In J. L. Matson (Ed.), *Applied Behavior Analysis for Children with Autism Spectrum Disorders* (pp. 237–57). New York: Springer.

Cain, K. and Dweck, C. S. (1995). The development of children's achievement, motivation patterns and conceptions of intelligence. *Merrill-Palmer Quarterly*, *41*, 25–52.

Carroll, J. J. and Steward, M. S. (1984). The role of cognitive development in children's understanding of their own feelings. *Child Development*, *55*, 1486–92.

Cassirer, E. (1953). *Philosophy of Symbolic Forms*. New Haven: Yale University Press.

Centre for Research and Innovations (2007). *Understanding the Brain: The Birth of a Learning Science*. OECD.

Chacko, A., Wymbs, B. T., Wymbs, F. A., Pelham, W. E., Swanger-Gagne, M. S., Girio, E., Pirvics, L., Herbst, L., Guzzo, J., Phillips, C. and O'Connor, B. (2009). Enhancing traditional behavioral parent training for single mothers of children with ADHD. *Journal of Clinical Child & Adolescent Psychology*, *38*, 206–18.

Chalmers, E. (2010). An exploration into the coping strategies of preschoolers: implications for professional practice. Master of Educational Psychology Research Project, University of Melbourne.

Chappell, K. and Young, S. (2007). *Report: Zest Project*. University of Exeter. Available at www.takeart.org/start/documents/Zestrep.pdf (accessed November 2009).

Clark, A. and Moss, P. (2001). *Listening to Children: The Mosaic Approach*. London: National Children's Bureau.

Coates, E. (2002). 'I forgot the sky' Children's stories contained within their drawings (Electronic version). *International Journal of Early Years Education*, *10*(1), 22–35.

Commonwealth of Australia. (2009). Belonging, being and becoming: the early years learning framework for Australia. A Document produced by the Australian Government Department of Education Employment and Workplace for the Council of Australian Governments.

Compas, B. E. (2009). Coping, regulations and development during childhood and adolescents. In E. A. Skinner and M. J. Zimmer-Gembeck (Eds), *Coping and the Development of Regulation. New Directions for Child and Adolescent Development*, pp. 87–99. San Francisco: Jossey-Bass.

Compas, B. E., Malcarne, V. L. and Fondacaro, K. M. (1988). Coping with stressful events in older children and young adolescents. *Journal of Consulting and Clinical Psychology*, *56*, 405–11.

Compas, B. E., Connor-Smith, J. K., Saltzman, H., Thomsen, A. H. and Wadsworth, M. E. (2001). Coping with stress during childhood and adolescence: problems, progress and potential in theory and research. *Psychological Bulletin, 127*(1), 87–128.

Cremin, H. and Slatter, B. (2004). Is it possible to access the 'voice' of pre-school children? Results of a research project in a pre-school setting. *Educational Studies, 30*(4), 458–70.

Csikszentmihalyi, M. (1990). *Flow: The Psychology of Optimal Experience*. New York: Harper & Row.

Day, P., Murphy, A. and Cooke, J. (1999). Traffic light lessons: problem-solving skills with adolescents. *Community Practitioner, 72*, 322–4.

Deans, J., Frydenberg, E., Tsurutani, H. (2010). Operationalising social and emotional coping competencies in kindergarten children 2010. *New Zealand Research in Early Childhood Education Journal, 13*, 113–24.

Denham, S. A., (1986). Social cognition, social behaviour and emotion in pre-schoolers: contextual validation. *Child Development, 57*, 194–201.

— (2006). Social-emotional competence as support for school readiness: what is it and how do we assess it? *Early Education & Development, 17*, 57–89.

Denham, S. A. and Burton, R. (2003). *Social and Emotional Prevention and Intervention Programming for Preschoolers*. New York: Springer.

Denham, S. A., Blair, K., De Mulder, E., Levitas, E., Sayer, K., Aurbach-Major S. and Queenan, P. (2003). Preschool emotional competence: pathway to social competence. *Child Development, 74*(1), 238–56.

Dewey, J. (1934). *Art as Experience*. New York: Capricorn Books.

Diem-Wille, G. (2001). A therapeutic perspective: the use of drawings in child psycho-analysis and social science. In T. van Leeuwen and C. Jewitt (Eds), *Handbook of Visual Analysis* (pp.119–33). London: Sage.

Diener, C. and Dweck, C. S. (1978). An analysis of learned helplessness: continuous changes in performance, strategy, and achievement cognitions following failure. *Journal of Personality and Social Psychology, 36*, 451–61.

— (1980). An analysis of learned helplessness: II. The processing of success. *Journal of Personality and Social Psychology, 39*, 940–52.

Diener, E. (2000). Subjective well-being: the science of happiness, and a proposal for a national index. *American Psychologist, 55*, 34–43.

Disque, J. G. and Langenbrunner, M. R. (1996). Shaping self concept with children's books. *Dimensions of Early Childhood, 24*, 5–9.

Docket, S. and Perry, B. (2005). Children's drawings: experiences and expectations of school (electronic version). *International Journal of Equity and Innovation in Early Childhood, 3*(2), 77–89.

Driessnack, M. (2006). Draw and tell conversations about fear. *Qualitative Health Research, 16*(10), 1414–35.

Durlak, J., Weissberg, R., Dymnicki, A., Taylor, R. E. and Schellinger, B. (2011). The impact of enhancing students' social and emotional learning: a meta-analysis of school-based universal interventions. *Child Development, 82*(1), 405–32.

Dweck, C. S. (1991). Self-theories and goals: their role in motivation, personality, and development. In R. Dienstbier (Ed.), *Nebraska Symposium on Motivation, Perspectives on Motivation. Current Theory and Research in Motivation* (Vol. 38, pp. 199–255). Lincoln, NE: University of Nebraska Press.

— (1998). The development of early self-conceptions: their relevance to motivational processes. In J. Heckhausen and C. S. Dweck (Eds), *Motivation and Self-Regulation across the Life-Span* (pp. 257–80). New York: Cambridge.

Dweck, C. S. and Leggett, E. (1988). A social-cognitive approach to motivation and personality. *Psychological Review, 95*, 256–73.

Dweck, C. S. and Sorich, L. (1999). Mastery-oriented thinking. In C. R. Snyder (Ed.), *Coping: The Psychology of What Works* (pp. 205–27). Oxford: Oxford University Press.

Ebata, A. T. and Moos, R. H. (1991). Coping and adjustment in distressed and healthy adolescents. *Journal of Applied Developmental Psychology, 12*, 33–54.

Edwards, C., Gandini, L. and Forman, G. (Eds) (1998). *The Hundred Languages of Children: The Reggio Emilia Approach to Early Childhood Education* (2nd edn). New Jersey: Ablex Publishing Corporation.

Eisenberg, N. and Fabes, R. A. (1998). Prosocial development. In W. Damon and N. Eisenberg (Eds), *Handbook of Child Psychology: Vol. 3. Social, Emotional, and Personality Development* (5th edn, pp. 701–78). Hoboken, NJ: Wiley.

Eisenberg, N., Fabes, R., Murphy, B., Maszek, P., Smith, M. and Karbon, M. (1995). The role of emotionality and regulation in children's social functioning: a longitudinal study. *Child Development, 66*, 109–28.

Eisenberg, N., Fabes, R. A. and Guthrie, I. (1997). Coping with stress: the roles of regulation and development. In J. N. Sandier and S. A. Wolchik (Eds), *Handbook of Children's Coping with Common Stressors: Linking Theory, Research, and Intervention* (pp. 41–70). New York: Plenum.

Eisenberg, N., Cumberland, A. and Spinrad, T. L. (1998). Parental socialization of emotion. *Psychological Inquiry, 9*, 241–73.

Eisner, E. (2002). *The Arts and the Creation of the Mind.* New Haven: Yale University Press.

Elliot, E. and Dweck, C. (1988). Goals: an approach to motivation and achievement. *Journal of Personality and Social Psychology, 54*, 5–12.

Emery, R. E. (1988). *Marriage, Divorce, and Children's Adjustment.* Beverly Hills: Sage.

Erikson, E. H. (1968). *Identity: Youth and Crisis.* New York: Norton.

— (1985). *The Life Cycle Completed.* New York: Norton.

Exiner, J. and Lloyd, P. (1973). *Teaching Creative Movement.* Sydney: Angus and Robertson.

— (1981). *Learning through Dance. A Guide for Teachers.* Melbourne: Oxford University Press.

Fields, L. and Prinz, R. J. (1997). Coping and adjustment during childhood and adolescence. *Clinical Psychology Review, 17*, 937–76.

Folkman, S. and Lazarus, R. S. (1980). An analysis of coping in a middle aged community sample. *Journal of Health and Social Behaviour, 21*, 219–39.

— (1985). If it changes it must be a process: a study of emotion and coping during three stages of a college examination. *Journal of Personality and Social Psychology, 48*(1), 150–70.

— (1988). The relationship between coping and emotion: implications for theory and research. *Social Science Medicine, 26*(3), 309–17.

Folkman, S., Lazarus, R. S., Pimley, S. and Novacek, J. (1987). Age differences in stress and coping. *Psychology and Aging, 2*(2), 171–84.

Freud, S. (1964). *An Outline of Psychoanalysis, the Standard Edition of the Complete Psychological Works of Sigmund Freud* (Vol. XXIII). London: Hogarth Press and the Institute of Psychoanalysis.

Frijda, N. H. (1993). Moods, emotions, episodes and emotions. In M. Lewis and J. M. Haviland (Eds), *Handbook of Emotions* (pp. 381–403). New York: Guilford.

Frydenberg, E. (1993). The coping strategies used by capable adolescents. *Australian Journal of Guidance & Counselling, 3*, 15–23.

— (2007). *Coping for Success. CD-Rom.* Melbourne: Australian Council for Educational Research.

— (2008). *Adolescent Coping: Advances in Theory, Research and Practice.* London: Routledge.

— (2010). *Think Positively: A Course for Developing Coping Skills in Adolescents.* London: Continuum.

Frydenberg, E. and Brandon, C. (2007a). *The Best of Coping: Facilitators Guide.* Melbourne: Australian Council for Educational Research.

— (2007b). *The Best of Coping: Student Workbook.* Melbourne: Australian Council for Educational Research.

Frydenberg, E. and Deans, J. (2011). *The Early Years Coping Cards.* Melbourne: Australian Council for Educational Research.

Frydenberg. E. and Lewis, R. (1993). *Manual: The Adolescent Coping Scale.* Melbourne: Australian Council for Educational Research.

— (1997). *Coping Scale for Adults.* Melbourne: Australian Council for Educational Research.

— (1999). Things don't get better just because you're older: a case for facilitating reflection. *British Journal of Educational Psychology, 69*, 83–96.

Frydenberg, E., Lewis, R., Kennedy, G., Ardila, R., Frindte, W. and Hannoun, R. (2003). Coping with concerns: an exploratory comparison of Australian, Colombian, German and Palestinian adolescents. *Journal of Youth and Adolescence, 32*, 59–66.

Gardner, H. (1983). *Frames of Mind: The Theory of Multiple Intelligences.* New York: Basic Books.

— (1994). Multiple intelligences theory. In R. J. Sternberg (Ed.), *Encyclopedia of Human Intelligence* (Vol. 2, pp. 740–2). New York: Macmillan.

Garner, P. W. and Estep, K. M. (2001). Toddlers' emotion regulation behaviors: the role of social context and family. *Journal of Genetic Psychology, 156*, 417–30.

Goleman, D. (1998). *Working with Emotional Intelligence.* London: Bloomsbury.

— (2005). *Emotional Intelligence.* 10th anniversary edition. New York: Bantam Books.

Gonzalez, N. (2001). *I Am My Language: Discourses of Women and Children in the Borderlands.* Tuscon, AZ: University of Arizona Press.

Graham, P. (1998). *Cognitive Behaviour Therapy for Children and Families.* Cambridge: Cambridge University Press.

Gray, C. (2001). *My Social Stories Book.* London: Jessica Kingsley.

Hade, D. (2002). Storyselling: are publishers changing the way children read? *The Horn Book Magazine*, 78.

Hampel, P. and Petermann, F. (2005). Age and gender effects on coping in children and adolescents. *Journal of Youth and Adolescence*, *34*(2), 73–83.

Hampton, T. (2006). The effects of stress on children examined. *Journal of the American Medical Association*, *295*(16), 1888.

Hanna, J. L. (1979). *To Dance is Human: A Theory of Non-verbal Communication*. Chicago: University of Chicago Press.

Harris, P. L. and Olthof, T. (1982). The child's concept of emotion. In G. Butterworth and P. Light (Eds), *Social Cognition: Studies of the Development of Understanding* (pp. 188–209). Chicago: University of Chicago Press.

Hauser, S. T. and Bowlds, M. K. (1990). Stress, coping, and adaptation. In S. S. Feldman and G. R. Elliott (Eds), *At the Threshold: The Developing Adolescent* (pp. 388–413). Cambridge, MA: Harvard University Press.

Heard, G. (1987). *For the Good of the Earth and the Sun: Teaching Poetry*. Portsmouth, NH: Heinemann.

Hedges, H. (2004). A lesson in listening and thinking: Katie and her shadow. *New Zealand Journal of Infant and Toddler Education*, *6*, 13–18.

Herbert, C. and Dweck, C. (1985). Mediators of persistence in preschoolers: implications for development. Unpublished manuscript, Harvard University.

Heyman, G., Dweck, C. and Cain, K. (1992). Young children's vulnerability to self-blame and helplessness. *Child Development*, *63*, 401–15.

Hiroto, S. S. and Seligman, M. E. (1975). Generality of learned helplessness in man. *Journal of Personality and Social Psychology*, *31*(2). 311–27.

Ho, Y.-C., Cheung, M.-C. and Chan, A. S. (2003). Music training improves verbal but not visual memory: cross-sectional and longitudinal explorations in children. *Neuropsychology*, *17*(3), 439–50.

Holliday, E., Harrison, L. J. and McLeod, S. (2009). Listening to children with communication impairment talking through their drawings. *Journal of Early Childhood Research*, *7*(3), 244–63.

Hubert, N. C., Jay, S. M., Saltoun. M. and Hayes, M. (1988). Approach-avoidance and distress in children undergoing preparation for painful medical procedures. *Journal of Clinical Child Psychology*, *17*, 194–202.

Izard, C. E. (1993). Organizational and motivational functions of discrete emotions. In M. Lewis and J. Haviland (Eds), *Handbook of Emotions* (pp. 631–41). New York: Guilford.

— (2002). Translating emotion theory and research into preventive interventions. *Psychological Bulletin*, *128*, 796–824.

Jung, C. G. (Ed.) (1964). *Man and His Symbols*. London: Aldus.

Kendrick, M. E. and McKay, R. (2009). Researching literacy with young children's drawings. In N. Narey (Ed.), *Making Meaning. Constructing Multimodal Perspectives of Language, Literacy, and Learning through Arts-Based Early Childhood Education* (pp. 53–70). New York: Springer.

Keyes, C. L. M. (2005). Mental illness *and/or* mental health? Investigating axioms of the Complete State Model of Health. *Journal of Consulting and Clinical Psychology*, *73*, 539–48.

Kliewer, W., Parrish, K. A., Taylor, K. W., Jackson, K., Walker, J. M. and Shivy, V. A. (2006). Socialization of coping with community violence: influences of caregiver coaching, modeling, and family context. *Child Development, 77*, 605–23.

Kopp, C. B. (2009). Emotion-focused coping in young children: self and self-regulatory processes. In E. A. Skinner and M. J. Zimmer-Gembeck (Eds), *Coping and the Development of Regulation*. A volume for the series, R. W. Larson and L. A. Jensen (Eds-in-Chief), *New Directions in Child and Adolescent Development*. San Francisco: Jossey-Bass.

Lavender, L. and Predcock-Linnell, J. (2001). From improvisation to choreography: The critical bridge. *Research in Dance Education, 2*(2), 195–209.

Lazarus, R. S. and Folkman, S. (1984). *Stress, Appraisal, and Coping*. New York: Springer.

Leonard, M. (2006). Children's drawings as a methodological tool: Reflections on the eleven plus system in Northern Ireland. *Irish Journal of Sociology, 15*(2), 52–66.

Lett, W. (1995). Experiential supervision through simultaneous drawing and talking. *The Arts in Therapy, 22*(4), 315–28.

Liew, J., Eisenberg, N., Losoya, S. H., Guthrie, I. K. and Murphy, B. C. (2003). Maternal expressivity as a moderator of the relations of children's vicarious emotional responses to their regulation, emotionality, and social functioning. *Journal of Family Psychology, 17*(4), 584–97.

Lobo, Y. B. and Winsler, A. (2006). The effects of a creative dance and movement program on the social competence of head start preschoolers. *Social Development, 15*(3) August 2006, 501–19.

McCutchen, B. Pugh. (2006). *Teaching Dance as Art in Education*. Champaign, IL: Human Kinetics.

McDonnell, J., Mathot-Buckner, C, Thorson, N. and Fister, S. (2001). Supporting the inclusion of student with moderate and severe disabilities in junior high school general education classes: the effects of classwide peer tutoring, multi-element curriculum, and accommodations. *Education and Treatment of Children, 24*, 141–60.

Malloch, S. N. (1999, 2000). Mothers and infants and communicative musicality. *Musicae Scientiae*, 29–57. Retrieved 6 March 2011 from www.heartmind.com.au/images/communicative_musicality_199–2000.pdf

Meltzoff, A. N. and Moore, M. K. (1977). Imitation of facial and manual gestures by human neonates. *Science, 198*, 75–8.

Mettler, B. (1979). *Materials of Dance: As a Creative Art Activity*. Tuscon, AZ: Mettler Studios.

Miller, W. R. and Seligman, M. E. P. (1975). Learned helplessness, depression, and the perception of reinforcement. *Behavior Research and Therapy, 14*, 7–17.

Napier, R. and Gershenfeld, M. (2004). *Groups: Theory and Experience*. Boston: Houghton Mifflin.

Neven, R. S. (1996). *Emotional Milestones: From Birth to Adulthood: A Psychodynamic Approach*. Australian Council for Educational Research.

Nicholson, J. and Pearson, Q. M. (2003). Helping children cope with fears: using children's literature in classroom guidance. *Professional School Counseling, 7*, 15–19.

Nimmo, J. (1993). Social competence: a pilot study of a cognitive-behavioural social skills program with comparisons of outcomes for in-class and withdrawal groups. Unpublished M.Ed. Thesis, Queensland University.

Papalia, D. E. and Olds, S. W. (1989). *Life Span Development* (1st Australian edition). Sydney: McGraw-Hill.

Pavri, S. and Luftig, R. L. (2000). The social face of inclusive education: are students with learning disabilities really included in the classroom? *Preventing School Failure, 45*, 8–14.

Pekrun, R., Goetz, T., Titz, W. and Perry, R. P. (2002). Academic emotions in students' self-regulated learning and achievement: A program of qualitative and quantitative research. *Educational Psychologist, 37*(2), 91–105.

Peterson, G. and Leigh, G. (1990). The family and social competence in adolescence. In T. Gullotta, G. Adams and R. Montemayer (Eds), *Developing Social Competency in Adolescence*. California: Sage.

Piaget, J. (1970). *Genetic Epistemology*. New York: Columbia University Press.

Pincus, D. B. and Friedman, A. G. (2004). Improving children's coping with everyday stress: transporting treatment interventions to the school setting. *Clinical Child and Family Psychology Review, 7*, 223–40.

Pintrich, P., Roeser, R. and DeGroot, E. (1994). Classroom and individual differences in early adolescents' motivation and self-regulated learning. *Journal of Early Adolescence, 14*, 139–61.

Piscitelli, B. and Anderson, D. (2001). Young children's perspectives of museums settings and experiences. *Museum Management and Curatorship, 19*, 269–82.

Pramling, N. (2009). Introducing poetry-making in early years education. *European Early Childhood Education Research Journal, 17*, 377–90.

Ptacek, J. T., Smith, R. E. and Zanas, J. (1992). Gender, appraisal, and coping: a longitudinal analysis. *Journal of Personality, 60*, 747–70.

Quinn, M. M., Mathur, S. R. and Rutherford, R. B. (1996). *Social Skills and Social Competence of Children and Youth: A Comprehensive Bibliography of Articles, Chapters, Books, and Programs*. Tempe, AZ: Arizona State University.

Raver, C. (2002). Emotions matter: making the case for the role of young children's emotional development for early school readiness. *Social Policy Report of the Society for Research in Child Development, 16*(3), 1–20.

Redfern, H. B. (1983). *Dance Art and Aesthetics* London: Dance Books.

Robinson, R. H. III and Rotter, J. C. (1991). Children's fears: towards a preventative model. *School Counsellor, 38*, 187–202.

Rollins, J. A. (2005). Tell me about it: drawing as a communication tool for children with cancer. *Journal of Pediatric Oncology Nursing, 22*(4), 203–21.

Russel, J. (1975). *Creative Dance in the Primary School* (2nd edn). Plymouth: Macdonald and Evans.

Ryff, C. D. and Keyes, C. L. (1995). The structure of psychological well-being revisited. *Journal of Personality and Social Psychology, 69*(4), 719–27.

Saarni, C. (1990). Emotional competence: how emotions and relationships become integrated. In R. Thompson (Ed.), *Nebraska Symposium on Motivation: Socio-emotional Development* (Vol. 36, pp. 115–82). Lincoln, NE: University of Nebraska Press.

Salovey, P. and Mayer, J. D. (1990). Emotional intelligence. *Imagination, Cognition, and Personality, 9*, 185–211.

Salovey, P., Bedell, B., Detweiler, J. B. and Mayer, J. D. (1999). Coping intelligently: emotional intelligence and the coping process. In C. R. Snyder (Ed.), *Coping: The Psychology of What Works* (pp. 141–64). New York: Oxford University press.

Sandler, I. N., Wolchik, S. A., MacKinnon, D., Ayers, T. S. and Roosa, M. W. (1997). Developing linkages between theory and intervention in stress and coping processes. In S. A. Wolchik and I. N. Sandler (Eds), *Handbook of Children's Coping: Linking Theory and Intervention* (pp. 3–41). New York: Plenum.

Seligman, M. E. P. and Csikszentmihalyi, M. (2000). Positive psychology: an introduction. *American Psychologist, 55*(1), 5–14.

Shulman, L. S. (1993). Teaching as community property: putting an end to pedagogical solitude. *Change, 25*(6), 6–7.

Simpson, R. L., Smith Myles, B., Sasso, G. M. and Kamps, D. M. (1991). *Social Skills for Students with Autism*. Reston, VA: Council for Exceptional Children.

Skewes, K. and Thompson, G. (1998). The use of musical interactions to develop social skills in early intervention. *The Australian Journal of Music Therapy, 9*, 35–44.

Skinner, E. A. and Zimmer-Gembeck, M. J. (2007). The development of coping. *Annual Review Psychology, 58*, 119–44.

Skinner, E. A. and Zimmer-Gembeck, M. J. (Eds) (2009). Challenges to the developmental study of coping. In *New Directions for Child and Adolescent Development* (pp. 1–21). San Francisco: Jossey-Bass.

Skinner, E. A., Edge, K. and Altman, J. and Sherwood, H. (2003). Searching for the structure of coping: a review and critique of category systems for classifying ways of coping. *Psychological Bulletin, 129*, 216–69.

Sloboda, J. and Deliege, I. (1996). *Musical Beginnings: Origins and Development of Musical Competence*. London: Oxford University Press.

Smith-Autard, J. M. (2004). *Dance Composition: A Practical Guide to Creative Success in Dance Making*. London: AC & Black.

Sorich, L. and Dweck, C. (1997). Psychological mediators of student achievement in transition to junior high school. Unpublished manuscript, Columbia University.

Sorin, R. (2005). *Who's Afraid of the Fire Alarm or of Going to Preschool? – A Comparative Study of Early Childhood Fears and Caregivers' Responses to Fear in Australia and in Canada*. Available at www.aare.edu.au/04pap/sor04018.pdf (accessed 16 March 2009).

State of Victoria (Department of Education and Early Childhood Development. (2009). Victorian Early Years Learning and Development Framework. Early Childhood Strategy Division of Department of Education and Early Childhood Development and Victorian Curriculum and Assessment Authority.

Steinberg, R. (2009). Heartsinger. *School Library Journal, 55*(3), 155–6.

Stinson, S. W. (1988). *Dance for Young Children: Finding the Magic in the Movement*. Reston, VA: American Alliance for Health, Physical Education, Recreation, and Dance.

Tsurutani, H. (2009). A multi-informant approach to understanding the coping behaviours of preschool children: a comparative study of teachers' and parents' observations. Master of Educational Psychology Research Project, University of Melbourne.

Tobin, D. L., Holroyd, K. A., Reynolds, R. V. C. and Wigal, J. K. (1989). The hierarchical factor structure of the coping strategies inventory. *Cognitive Therapy and Research, 13,* 343–61.

Trehub, S. E. (2001). Musical predispositions in infancy. *Annals of the New York Academy of Sciences, 930,* 1–16.

Trevarthen, C. (2002). Origins of musical identity: Evidence from infancy for musical social awareness. In R. A. R. MacDonald, D. J. Hergreaves and D. Miell (Eds), *Musical Identities* (pp. 21–38). Oxford: Oxford University Press.

Trevarthen, C. and Malloch, S. (2002). Musicality and music before three: human vitality and invention shared with pride. *Zero to Three, 23,* 10–17.

Trousdale, A. (1989). Who is afraid of the big bad wolf? *Children's Literature in Education, 20,* 69–79.

UNCRC. (1989). Convention on the Rights of the Child. Geneva: Office of the United Nations High Commissioner of Human Rights.

Valiente, C., Fabes, R. A., Eisenberg, N. and Spinrad, T. L. (2004). The relations of parental expressivity and support to children's coping with daily stress. *Journal of Family Psychology, 18*(1), 97–106.

Vasey, M. W. (1993). Development and cognition in childhood anxiety. The example of worry. *Advances in Clinical Child Psychology, 15,* 1–39.

von Georgi, R., Gobel, M. and Gebhardt, S.(2006). Emotion modulation by means of music and coping behaviour. In R. Hass and V. Brandes (Eds), *Music That Works. Contributions of Biology, Neurophysiology, Psychology, Sociology, Medicine and Musicology* (pp. 301–19). New York: Springer Wien.

Vygotsky, L. (1962). *Thought and Language.* Cambridge, MA: MIT Press.

—(1986). *Thought and Language.* Cambridge, MA, and London: Massachusetts Institute of Technology.

Wallerstein, J. S. and Lewis, J. M. (2004). The unexpected legacy of divorce. Report of a 25 year study. *Psychoanalytic Psychology, 21*(3), 353–70.

Wilmshurst, L. (2008). *Abnormal Child Psychology: A Developmental Perspective.* New York: Routledge.

Wright, S. (2003). *The Arts. Young Children, and Learning.* Boston, MA: Pearson Education.

Youngs, B. B. (1985). *Stress in Children: How to Recognise, Avoid and Overcome It.* New York: Arbor House.

Zhao, W., Dweck, C. and Mueller, C. (1998). Implicit theories and vulnerability to depression-like responses. Manuscript submitted for publication.

Zins, J., Bloodworth, M., Weissberg, R. and Walberg, H. (2004). The scientific base linking social and emotional learning to school success. In J. Zins, R. Weissberg, M. Wang and H. J. Walberg (Eds), *Building Academic Success on Social and Emotional Learning: What Does the Research Say?* (pp. 1–22). New York: Teachers Press, Columbia University.

Index